# CHRISTIANITY AT ITS BEST

*For Sinead, Eoin and Eva*

Donal Harrington

# Christianity at Its Best

BELIEVING AND BELONGING

the columba press

First published in 2012 by
ᴛʜe coʟᴜᴍʙᴀ ᴘʀᴇss
55A Spruce Avenue, Stillorgan Industrial Park,
Blackrock, Co Dublin

Cover by Bill Bolger
Origination by The Columba Press
Printed by Sprint-Print Ltd

ISBN 978 1 85607 760 6

Second Printing, 2014

# Contents

# Introduction

'Always be ready to give an answer to people who ask you the reason for the hope that is in you' (1 Peter 3:15). Christianity is about hope. I, like many others, have been touched by that hope. This book is offered in the spirit of sharing the hope and articulating something of the reason for it.

So the book is about Christianity. Just what is it that Christians believe? What is the heart of Christianity? What does it say about the big questions in life? What is the Christian way of living life? The book seeks to articulate something inspiring about Christianity at its best.

That last phrase suggests that there is a difference between Christianity at its best and Christianity as it actually is. Some people call it the difference between Christianity and church; what was meant to be and what we have ended up with. In recent times, in this part of the world, people sense a gap between the institution of church and the originating spirit that is still experienced in local communities.

This reminds me of looking in a mirror. When you look in a mirror you see yourself as you are. But you may also see what is not there. You may sense what is missing. You may glimpse yourself as you can be. In a similar way I am trying to give expression to Christianity as it can be, as it is meant to be. There is so much more to it, and to the hope that it offers.

In that sense the book is idealistic. It seeks to be as positive as it can be about Christianity at its best. In being idealistic it is also questioning. It questions what is there in the mirror when we look at church. I have in mind ways of thinking that are outdated and antiquated. I am thinking of the caricature that is out there of what Christians believe. I am thinking of how 'church' gets Christianity wrong.

So the book is written in a spirit of what I call critical loyalty. It does not claim to present the 'party line', the official view on the topics it discusses. It attempts to be loyal to the core of what Christianity is about. In doing so it is critical of how that core can become obscured. Thus, critical loyalty is for the sake of Christianity and for the sake of the church.

I think that nothing less will do today. When we are in the
middle of something it can be hard to see things in perspective.
It does seem, though, that Christianity is in serious decline in
this part of the world. Believing (at least in the sense of 'religion') is seen as passé. It is not seen as relevant, it does not connect. Partly it is the times we live in, partly it is the church itself.

In that kind of crisis, to continue with the *status quo* means
being headed for extinction. What is required is to reach back in.
What is required is for Christianity to rediscover its own heart,
for Christians to reconnect with the hope that is within them. As
they do, they may also reconnect in a creative way with people
in their spiritual journey today.

As I was writing the book, I found that it divided itself into
three sections. The first of these is about the 'shape' of Christian
belief. It asks, what kind of faith is Christian faith? I acknowledge here that faith and God and grace are bigger than
Christianity; they are universally accessible. In that context I
present the core of Christianity as revolving around Jesus – who
he was and what Christians believe he is today.

The second section is about questions we ask. It presents a
Christian perspective on big questions in life such as suffering,
sin and death. It also looks into big questions about Christianity
itself, such as its relationship to other religions and its views
about women. Here I am seeking to offer refreshing perspectives, to move beyond obsolete ways of thinking into new ways
of seeing.

In section three I paint a picture of how Christianity is lived –
some of the practical aspects of living life as a Christian. The
main focus is on putting the Christian call into practice in daily
life. I talk about both prayer and action. I emphasise the place of
the Christian community in the life of each Christian. This section is intended to be a kind of portrait of what adult faith looks
like.

Who is the book for? I come from the Catholic tradition but I
think most of it is about matters that all Christians have in common. In writing I was thinking of people who, while baptised,
might not have strong links with church and organised religion.
I hope they will find here an informative and attractive presentation of what Christianity is all about.

I was thinking too of people who are churchgoers. Perhaps they are people who sense the gap between Christianity and church. Or perhaps they are people who would like to update or refresh their understanding of what they believe. But for all, I hope the book helps to put words on the reasons Christians have for the hope that is in them.

CHAPTER ONE

# *Setting the Scene*

The aim of the book is to give a positive presentation for today of what Christianity is all about. This first chapter is about the 'today'. It sets the scene for what follows by sketching what is happening to faith and belief in today's culture. Such a sketch is no easy task and there are differing views on the matter. So I am going to suggest the following scenario as a way into the topic.

*Imagine*

Imagine that we have assembled a group of what we will call 'reasonably-minded people' to discuss what is happening to faith and belief today. The group will include people with different perspectives and different convictions. But they will be reasonably minded, which means that they should be able to come up with conclusions that other reasonably-minded people could go along with.

So, if asked the question, 'what is happening to faith and belief in today's culture?', what would that group come up with? I think it would be balanced, meaning that they would steer somewhere in between extreme views. So, on the one hand, they would hardly come up with a disparaging rejection of faith and religion. On the other hand, they would hardly come up with a triumphalist affirmation of religion as we have known it.

What they agree on would probably include the following. First, they would agree that something huge has changed as regards religion (at least in Europe; other parts of the world are quite different). Its positioning in society has changed dramatically in recent centuries. It has gone from a central place of dominance and is heading towards a marginal place of inconsequence.

This might lead them into asking; if this is the case, then has religion had its day? They would probably find it harder to agree about this. Certainly in the past, believing was, as it were, the 'default mode' of society, while today it is increasingly the case that not believing is the default mode. But would the group be unanimous in concluding that this spells the end of religion?

What they might concur about is that something of religion as we knew it has certainly died. I am thinking of the superstitious, magical kind of religion that sees mysterious forces working everywhere and seeks to manipulate them by prayers and ritual. While that kind of consciousness is still alive, they might agree that, as a worldview, it has been superseded by our scientific knowledge.

The group might also talk about the kind of religion that is characterised by authoritarianism and control of people's spiritual lives. They might talk too about fanatical forms of religion. Both of these are still very much in evidence, but our 'reasonably-minded' people would hardly enthuse about them. They would probably worry, though, that they will not disappear in the foreseeable future.

At the same time, our group might come to see that much of today's reaction against religion is a reaction against this kind of religion. They might discuss the anger, the hurt, the resentment, the intolerance there is in relation to religion. But they would also ask themselves the question; are these feelings a reaction to religion as such or are they a reaction to certain distorted forms of religion?

Next, they might agree that, whatever about religion, there is something that has not died or had its day. In the 1960s there were books about 'the death of God'; but it would seem that God did not die. If anything the opposite has been the case. There has been a resurgence of things spiritual that was quite unexpected, unpredicted. We call it 'spirituality' today and it takes a staggering variety of forms, both weird and wonderful, both with a God and without a God.

What would our group make of this? They might talk about the distinction between 'spirituality' and 'religion' that is in currency today. If so, they would probably ask whether, in the future, we will have spirituality without religion? Or will this 'outbreak' of spirituality itself die out and give way to general unbelief? Or will there always be a spiritual hunger in people that leads them to look beyond what our technological and consumerist society can offer?

At any rate, the group finds itself left with a kind of paradox. Clearly, as regards religion, something has gone. But equally clearly, something has persisted. They find themselves left wondering …

*Reflecting Further*

I want to move on from this imagined scenario to offer some further reflections. It seems to me that what has happened is that people's relationship to organised religion and its beliefs has changed in a significant way. People are in a new place in their attitude or disposition towards religion.

In times when religion was dominant (I am thinking particularly of the Catholic Church), people were expected to accept it on its own terms – 'lock, stock and barrel'. It had its comprehensively worked-out system of beliefs and code of behaviour. The believer's role was simply to acquiesce. While there was talk of 'conscience', in reality people were not expected to think for themselves. It was a case of 'doctor knows best'.

But people have changed. As it was expressed somewhere, we have moved from 'the experience of authority' to 'the authority of experience'. People's experience of religion in the past was an experience of authority. But, more and more, people have come to trust in the wisdom of their own experience, their inner wisdom. That gives them a kind of inner yardstick for measuring what religion proposes to them. People come to religion from the authority of their own experience.

If so, how do people today judge religion? No doubt, different criteria are at work in different people. Where one person might want a good feeling, another might seek a challenge. What is going on throughout is that people are asking: how, if at all, might religion fit into my world? How will it contribute to my life's project? Previously they were expected to fit themselves into its world, but now the roles are reversed.

Possibly the pervasive criterion today, if not generally articulated so sharply, is this. People look at religion and ask: will religion make me more human or less human? That is a fearsome question for religion to answer. This is certainly so for Christianity, whose founder proclaimed: 'I came that they may have life and have it to the full' (John 10:10). It is an index of how things have gone off-course that people could be asking such a question of a religion grounded in such a promise.

It should also be noted that people are asking the same question of the world we live in today. For all our progress – all our science and technology, all our power and achievements – the promise of a bright new world has disappointed. We live in a capitalist-dominated world which is quite unfriendly, not just to believing, but even to human beings becoming fully human.

Perhaps it is the case that people are disappointed on both fronts, by their culture as well as by religion. People are searching for what we might call fullness of life. For many this 'fullness' has some transcendent reference; it reaches beyond. But very often it is a lonely search. People feel thrown back on their own resources, between a religion that does not connect with them and a culture that is not interested in them.

The language we are using, about fullness and becoming more human, is essentially 'spiritual' language. This is an important point, but it needs to be teased out, as the words 'spiritual' and 'spirituality', while so much in vogue today, are quite undefined. They can mean so many things that they almost mean nothing.

I recall a mother talking on a radio chat show about her adult daughter, who had died tragically. She said: 'I'm not saying that she was a saint, but she was a brilliant human being.' I found myself wondering what the difference is between the two. Being 'a brilliant human being' is what matters in life. But that is what spirituality is all about – being and becoming more human, fullness of life.

What the 'spiritual' language brings out is the sense that being a human being has depth. It is bathed in meaning and value. It reaches beyond the banal and the everyday and the material. It touches on something that inspires commitment and loyalty and ecstasy. Fullness of life has a 'more' to it. For a given individual, that may or may not include a 'God' aspect. But, with or without a God, it is what we have in common.

Unfortunately, the word 'religion' seems to be about something other than this human flourishing. At the same time people, in their spiritual journey or searching or hunger, will engage with organised religion if it offers some promise of enhancing the journey, enlightening the search, nourishing the hunger. If we say that religion is in decline today, we are saying that many do not perceive it as being able to contribute in that way.

*Christianity*

So, we live in a part of the world where religion is waning and where spirituality seems to be on the rise. But in this world the question of Christianity remains to be resolved. Is it part of what has had its day? Is it part of what is resurgent? Is Christianity more like 'religion' or more like 'spirituality'? Is it about promoting a discredited product or about recovering something of enduring value?

The key point, I suggest, is to distinguish between the core of a religion and the different forms it takes in different times. This captures where Christianity is at in this part of the world. Something certainly is dying, but it is actually an opportunity for Christianity to connect again with its own core and to make new sense to people. Maybe the decline in religion is welcome if the opportunity is taken, to let go of forms that no longer serve and get back to what really matters.

Another thought about the words 'religion' and 'spirituality'. The word religion used to have the meaning, not of an institution, but of a disposition or attitude towards the Mystery – a mood of awe, of wonder, of reverence. And the word spirituality also has an older meaning. It used to refer specifically to Christianity, to the practices and disciplines and dynamics of living a Christian life.

This says that Christianity is all about what we call spirituality, even though it may be perceived as something to which spirituality is an alternative. It also suggests that, in turning from religion to spirituality, people may actually be holding on to what is at the heart of all religion. The question then for Christianity is; can it recover its heart and be again what it is meant to be?

*For reflection*

Think of yourself in your spiritual search for fullness of life. How might church or organised religion be good for you in that search? How might it be bad for you? How might the western capitalist culture we live in be good for you in your search? How might it be bad for you?

CHAPTER TWO

## *Universal Grace*

The first step I want to take in understanding Christianity is to take the focus off Christianity itself and to focus instead on the world we live in. The first step is to appreciate that Christianity finds itself in a world that is already God's world.

There is a version of Christian religion that says 'outside the church no salvation'. The phrase itself goes back to the early centuries of Christianity and it meant something quite different then. But what it came to mean is as stark as it sounds; if you are not part of the (Catholic) Church you are not saved. What I will be saying here is very different.

### Grace

The thinking behind the phrase as usually understood goes like this. People need God's grace to save them from sin. That grace was given to us in Christ and is 'dispensed' to us by the church, particularly through its sacraments. It is like somebody having sole distribution rights over a product. The church appears here as having a monopoly on access to God's grace.

This monopolising tendency can be a feature of religion. It is not always the case, but religion can come at people with the message: 'We have what you need – and nobody else has.' However unintentional, there is an arrogance about that kind of religion, with the implicit claim of being the possessor of absolute truth.

But there is no monopoly. Truth and God and grace are bigger than all of us. Grace is something we all participate in, not something any of us possesses in some exclusive way. And 'God' is bigger than what any religion can contain. In the words of John's gospel, the Spirit blows where it will (John 3:8). We cannot box God in or control God, anymore than we can the wind.

Access is universal. There is no entry door barring access to God and grace other than the door of a person's heart. This in fact is the true Christian teaching, which has been obscured by the mindset of 'outside the church no salvation'. Grace is everywhere available, universally on offer to humankind.

It is worth pausing here to think about the words I have been using, 'God' and 'grace'. We have tended in the past to think about grace as an almost quantifiable 'thing', a commodity which God gives us. Receiving it bestows on us certain privileges, such a being in 'the state of grace'; without it we are lost. We even spoke of different kinds of grace – actual grace, sanctifying grace, and so on.

Today we think differently. Today grace is understood simply as God's giving of God's self. To bring that down to earth, think about the difference between giving money to somebody and giving them our time. Giving money can be easier, because giving time requires giving of ourselves in a way that giving money does not. Indeed, the best present is the one where we feel the gift of the person's own self.

## Life

Likewise, what God gives us is nothing other than God. So, where or when do we experience this gift of God's own self? The answer, I propose, is life itself. Life, given to us before any request of ours, is the gift *par excellence* wherein we may come to experience the gift of the giver's own self.

Many years ago, the Irish theologian James Mackey wrote a book which he titled *Life and Grace*. Looking back some time later, he is reported to have said that, were he writing it again, he would change the title to *Life is Grace*. It is not that life is one thing and grace another thing added to it. Life itself is the grace. Life is imbued with God's own self-giving. Life is imbued with God's Spirit, as the air is with the wind.

I prefer this way of looking at things to the one that sees grace more like supernatural forces at work in the world – either the divinity intervening in inscrutable ways, or our imploring divine interventions. Instead of that, I suggest that life itself is the divine intervention and its every moment can be experienced as gift, as grace.

We are talking here about an experience of grace that is bigger than religion. It is not that grace is something added on (by religion) to a life that is not already grace. Life is already grace. Grace is not an alien substance, but a natural, native, inherent quality of life itself. In a truly Christian view of things, life cannot be imagined as being other than graced.

Think again of the word 'grace'. It has connotations of something agreeable, elegant, charming. Think, for example, of a dance or movement that is graceful. Or think of being graced with somebody's presence. But it is also the same root word as the word 'grateful'. To say that life is grace, or that grace is everywhere, is to say that life has those kind of qualities. It is to say that the life we live invites us to be appreciative.

As I write, I am also thinking of the opposite, of the person who would curse life rather than be grateful. To speak of life as grace does not mean that all in the garden is rosy. If it did, then nobody would be thankful. As it is, the people who are most thankful about life are not always the ones who have been luckiest. They are often people who have known the dark side of life and people who have inhabited pain.

*Ordinary and extraordinary*

Let me suggest some examples of how life is experienced as grace. Some years ago, I was teaching in a theology course and I asked the students for examples of 'religious experiences'. One of them spoke of a relation going to Lourdes and experiencing a cure. Another spoke of a strange happening once in the house, where candles began to move on the mantelpiece.

I commented: if this is what religious experience is, then it is quite out of the ordinary and unlikely to ever have anything to do with us. So I asked them if they could come up with examples more in the mainstream of real life. One student talked of a tragedy that had happened in the family. Another spoke of their granny's death. That was certainly getting more real, but it was all about tragic events. Then more examples came forth: one was the birth of a sister's baby; another was falling in love and getting married.

In the end we thought that 'spiritual experience' might be a better term than 'religious', but even that could be misleading. It could have us thinking of experiences that are outside the range of life as it is ordinarily lived. This would be as if our human life is one thing and then things 'spiritual' are other than this. It would be the same as what I just said about grace being thought of as added on to life.

Teilhard de Chardin, the Jesuit scientist and theologian, made the point in the following way: 'We are not human beings having a spiritual experience; we are spiritual beings having a human experience.' To say that life is grace is to say that we are spiritual beings. What makes us spiritual is the giftedness of life. And because we are spiritual we can experience life, our 'human' life, at depth.

There is a depth to life. There is a depth to ourselves. There is a 'more'. Life opens out onto something further. It is not closed in and entire of itself. We ourselves open onto a 'more'. It is not that there is ordinary life on one hand and things spiritual or religious on the other. It is that the ordinary has an extraordinary quality. And it is waiting for us to connect with it.

With this perspective we can easily add to the examples above. We could think of our experience of our children. We could think of the breath-taking quality music can have. We could think of our feelings of guilt. We could think of our sense of sublime beauty in the world. We could think of times when mortality invaded our minds. We could think of how we have at times surpassed ourselves. We could think of love.

Any of us can add to these examples once the point is grasped. The point is how ordinary they are. They are the stuff of life; they are the moments that await us around every corner. And the point is how extraordinary they are. They are windows into wonder, openings onto amazement. Because these two go together, the ordinary and the extraordinary, we say that life is grace.

To speak of spiritual experiences is not to speak of a different category of experiences, relatively rare and out of the ordinary. It is to speak, rather, of a dimension within ordinary, everyday human experience. We may not even mention words like God. We may just be talking about our children, our plans, the events of the day; and yet our talk may be full of faith and hope, of thanks and prayer.

In the past the 'spiritual' might have been associated almost exclusively with 'religion'. What is happening today is that, as religion has become more remote, people are connecting with the spiritual in a new way. This is not surprising, when we think that the spiritual is part of what we are as human beings.

# CHAPTER TWO    19

Religion might be experienced as something alien, imposed, but
this is different. To experience life in this way is to be in touch
with who we are.

But it is possible that we may not experience life in this way.
We may live life on the surface. These moments may pass us by.
We are not alive to their grace, or else only rarely and fleetingly.
If that is so, then we are not in touch with ourselves in the way
we might be. It reminds me of a phrase I heard: 'The distance be-
tween me and God is the distance between me and myself'.

## Thanks

I said that grace and thanks go together, as in the word 'grateful'. But gratitude is interpersonal. It is more than the 'thank
your lucky starts' we might feel in avoiding a misfortune. It implies one to whom we are thankful. It is akin to when we tell a
child to say thanks for a present; we are pointing beyond the gift
to the giver. To experience life as grace is to feel cause for
thanks. That feeling is already orienting us towards 'God'.

This echoes what I said in the last chapter about the word religion. Religion originally meant a personal disposition, not an
organisation. It meant a disposition of awe, of wonder, of reverence. A feeling of gratitude is part of this same complex of feelings. When we experience life as grace we are in touch with the
mystery, in a way that evokes these feelings.

That is why our understanding of Christianity begins here:
because this is where all religion begins. The starting point is
about God in the world and how that is experienced. In the way
I have put it, God is in the world as the grace of life itself, given
as a gift to be explored and appreciated, drawing us deeper into
the mystery of what it is to be a human being.

This in turn leads into asking about religions in the usual
sense of organised religion. Religions are about 'organising' this
experience in some way, that is, ritualising it, celebrating it, cop-
ing with it, clarifying it. More than anything else perhaps, they
are about bringing into clear focus the source of the grace, which
we usually call 'God'.

The trouble is that religions can easily become reduced to
something less than this. They can be reduced to controlling
grace and controlling us. But their true role is to facilitate us, to

make it easier for us to attend to the grace, to recognise it and appreciate it, to respond to it and live in it. This is where religions make their contribution. They are not the source of grace, in control of its distribution. Their role is to point to the source.

A later chapter will take up the question of the relationship between Christianity and other religions, the question of how Christianity sees itself in relation to them. The focus of this chapter has been on what is greater than all religions, the God who is universally present to humanity.

*For reflection*
Make a list of some of the experiences in your life where you have found yourself open to the 'more'. Think of times, be they good or bad, when life has led you to be thankful.

CHAPTER THREE

# *Faith*

When we appreciate that grace is bigger than Christianity, it leaves us in a position where we can appreciate better what Christianity is. The same is true of faith. In order to understand what Christian faith is, it will help if we first acknowledge the broader sense of what it means to believe.

Faith is bigger than Christianity, bigger than any religion. It is not that somebody has either Christian faith or no faith. This can appear to be the case when people talk about 'the faith'. Rather, everybody believes; the question is, what do they believe? Faith is part of being human, long before Christianity comes into the picture.

This deserves to be emphasised because of an impression that is abroad today about faith. The impression is that belief is irrational. It is felt that it is a suspension of a person's critical faculties. Faith is felt to be subjective, emotional, superstitious perhaps. It is seen as unenlightened, a failure or a refusal to grow up.

Also, in relation to the church, faith has a further connotation of blind obedience. It can suggest uncritical acceptance of the party line on a wide range of issues. It carries little sense of an invitation to think critically. Indeed it seems that people are expected to sacrifice their own rational convictions if they find themselves in conflict with the church's position.

Later on I will come back to that point. But for now, we leave Christianity aside and we reflect on faith as part of ordinary human life. Faith, or believing, is something that everybody is engaged in, not just those we call 'believers'. And this faith has two essential qualities. It is a rational, critically-minded activity. And it is a leap.

## Living is believing

The scientific mentality can tempt us into thinking that, if something cannot be proven, then it is not true. If it cannot be scientifically verified, it does not count as a fact. However, the fact is that a lot of our daily living is about believing. We survive on the basis of what we believe, more than on the basis of what we know for a fact. That is the way things are.

For instance, when I look at a signpost and it says to go straight on, I believe. When I read in the paper that the match starts at 4.00 pm, I believe. When the TV documentary tells me that X is the biggest-selling pharmaceutical product in the world, I believe. When the air-traffic controller tells the pilot: 'You are free to land', the pilot believes. And so on; so much of what we take as facts are beliefs. It may be possible to prove them, but there is not enough time. We are happy to believe.

Now let us move it to a more personal level. I trust in somebody else's word, be it friend, family member, colleague. More deeply, when you say 'I'll be there', or 'I love you'; I believe you, I trust you. So much of what is most important to us is taken on trust. This fabric of trust is a big part of our inter-relating as human beings.

But it is not blind trust or blind belief. It is rational. We seek out and weigh the evidence, we look for indications. We would be foolish not to. But we also take a leap. This is in contrast to the credulous person who would believe anything and does not take a critical stance. And it is in contrast to the overly cautious person who is too wary or suspicious ever to take a leap.

Then there is 'believing in'. For instance, do I believe in myself? Partly it is a matter of gathering the evidence about myself. But there is also a leap. Or again, there is my believing in you. We know how our believing in one another can be so transformative in our relationships.

These reflections on believing point also to an element of commitment. There is a commitment involved in my believing in you. Likewise there is my commitment to a cause that I believe in; a cause such as world peace, or respect for the environment, or equal dignity for all. There are values involved, the values I believe in, that inspire my commitment and guide my living.

If all this is true, then there is something about human life that transcends rational calculation. I do not mean that it is replaces our being rational, because that 'something' includes a high level of thinking and reflection and analysis. But it goes further. The leap of trust or commitment has a quality that is not reducible to the rational alone.

While believing may begin in childhood, it does not end

there. It does not disappear as we get older; rather it gets different. It incorporates our emerging rational capacities. It ceases to be credulous and becomes critical. Instead of being discarded it grows up.

*All are believers*

Next, consider a particular kind of 'believing in', namely, what it is that a person believes in most fundamentally. I am thinking of a person's basic 'position' as to what life or existence is all about. Some people will have pursued this question more attentively and more explicitly than others. But it is a question that occupies us all in one way or another.

I like the line that says: 'We are all caught up as actors in a drama we do not really understand.' It captures the situation we are all in. And we are all, in our way, trying to come to grips with it. In our minds and hearts we are trying to compose the picture, to fit the pieces together, to grasp the pattern. We make what we can of it; confusion gives way to some clarity – but never full clarity. In the end we make a leap as to what it is all about.

As an illustration of how somebody put the pieces together, take this passage from the Book of Wisdom in the Bible (chapter two):

> By chance we came to birth,
> and after this life we shall be as if we had never been.
> The breath in our nostrils is a puff of smoke,
> reason a spark from the beating of our hearts;
> put this out and our body turns to ashes
> and the spirit melts away like empty air …
> Come then, let us enjoy what good things there are …
> let not one flower of springtime pass us by.
> Let us leave the signs of our enjoyment everywhere,
> because this is our portion, the lot assigned us.

Obviously this is not the Bible's last word on the topic. But it is a stance, a position about the meaning of things, one that is quite common. We can see the evidence that points towards it. At the same time, it cannot be proven. Evidence can be adduced for the opposite position also, that life has a direction and is full of meaning. But neither can that be proven. There is a leap.

I think of the term 'atheist' here, which is usually contrasted with the term 'believer'. 'Atheist' means not believing in God. Unfortunately, that only tells us what the person is not. What we would like to hear more about is what the atheist does believe in! Because we all believe in something. We are all trying to make sense of things, we are all trying to figure out just what to believe about it all. It is part of being a human being.

We all take a stance. That there is a God; that there is nothing. That life has this meaning; or that meaning; or no meaning. That what matters most in life is this, or that. Whichever it may be, there is something that matters. So it is not satisfactory to divide people into believers and unbelievers. It makes more sense to think in terms of the different beliefs and commitments that people have about life and its meaning.

There is a striking expression of this in the novel, *The Life of Pi*, where the protagonist talks about the relationship he had with a teacher at college:

> He became my favourite teacher at Petit Séminaire … I felt a kinship with him. It was my first clue that atheists are my brothers and sisters of a different faith, and every word they speak speaks of faith. Like me, they go as far as the legs of reason will carry them – and then they leap.[1]

In a sense, it takes faith to be an atheist! The only one who does not take a leap is the agnostic, the one who stops at saying: 'I don't know.' And it is also possible to be a credulous atheist. Atheists no less than believers can fail to challenge themselves to think things through.

But presuming the person does think it through, a variety of positions about life's meaning are both possible and reasonable. The reason for this is that the evidence available to us is ambiguous. It does not point unequivocally to any particular conclusion. 'Two who look through prison bars; one sees the mud, the other the stars.'

Our experience of life is mixed. There is the sublime and there is the vulgar. On the one hand there is self-sacrificing love, on the other the self-interest that obeys no law. There is suffering that makes no sense and there is joy that is ecstatic. And so on. We each make our own sense of the mix. And that is our faith.

It could be that a person's experience of life, or their observation of life, is full of negativity; yet they come to a faith that affirms meaning. Meanwhile, another person may have had a very fortunate life, or may have encountered much that is dear; yet they end up believing that there is no point in it all.

And the ambiguities do not go away. A person may come to a particular position about things, but the questions do not stop. There is always the presence of conflicting evidence, alternative viewpoints. Whatever our beliefs, and however sure we feel about our beliefs, there is always something provisional. Life is about living with our unanswered questions.

Somebody said that atheism is the salt which preserves faith from corruption. I take this in the sense that we all have in us a curious mixture of believing and doubting, whether we are so-called 'atheists' or so-called 'believers'. That is our state in life and it is also our possibility for immersing ourselves further in the drama of life. We are not to suppress either our doubting or our believing.

*Faith*
Maybe, though, we should retain the word 'faith' for something more specific than this universal believing. Let us say, then, that all are believers, in the sense that all take their stance regarding the ultimate meaning of things, and that this stance is both rational and a leap. And within this view, let us take the word faith to refer to a particular kind of stance.

What I am thinking of here is seeing faith as a stance of ultimate trust. It is a position of trust or confidence regarding the ultimate meaning of life. It is the view, or the inclination to believe, that the universe is friendly and 'on our side'. Faith in this sense is very close to hope.

This kind of faith may or may not mention God. It could be shared by church-goers and by people who do not subscribe to a religion. It can be the stance of people who feel there is a God and of people who do not. And it is not an abstract theory or intellectual position. It is more action-centred and value-based.

Think of somebody whose living revolves around love for their family. Think of somebody who abhors injustice and deceit, who lives by values of integrity and solidarity. Think of someone who has journeyed from absorbed self-interest to other-centredness. Think of someone who, in the presence of suffering, has discovered within themselves hitherto dormant qualities of compassion and generosity.

Such values and loves and commitments are a kind of 'womb'. They are like a womb in the sense that they beget in the person a hope that there is something that gives enduring substance to their commitment. It might never be formulated as such, but it seems that, as such commitment grows deeper, the more it is permeated by a faith, a trust, a hope. That is why, I think, that this 'basic' kind of faith often, but not necessarily, opens out onto some sense of an ultimate, a sense of something more than ourselves, however it is articulated.

I have said that the opposite kind of stance – that the universe is indifferent or meaningless – is also reasonable. But perhaps it might be argued that the 'faith' I am describing, this sense of basic trust or confidence, is what our hearts most intimately tend towards. There is in us a 'thrust towards trust'. I see this as linking in with the topic of the last chapter, the sense of life as grace.

It may be the case today that there are many people who tend towards such basic trust, but for whom faith in a God is a somewhat separate question. Could it be that 'God' means the only version of God they ever had access to? Could it be that their basic trust is edging them in the direction of something resembling 'God'? Could it be that the God that is hinted at is quite vague and undefined?

Likewise, is it possible that some of those who explicitly confess to a God have yet to connect with the kind of faith or basic trust being spoken of here? It seems to me that it is possible that faith in God can exist separately from a person's feelings about life. It is possible to have 'the faith' without 'faith'. It is possible to remain in a childhood mode of faith and never to embark on the search or live with the uncertainties or experience the blessing of unresolved questions.

Later in this section I will take up the topic of Christian faith. The point here is to say that faith as such is much broader than religion. It is about a universal human activity of making sense of our situation. Christian faith is about what happens when the 'believer' in that sense encounters Christianity. Christianity is not so much about a person arriving at faith. It is about a person of faith – whatever form the leap has taken in their case – arriving at Christianity.

*For reflection*
Thinking of people you know, what would you say to the idea that there is a lot of faith in people's hearts, whether or not God is actually mentioned?

CHAPTER FOUR

# *Who was Jesus?*

As a prelude to talking about Christianity, I have been painting a picture of a world where grace is already active, where God is experienced in ways apart from Christianity. The question now is: amidst this rich diversity, what is the specific nature of Christianity? The question is not about something better or superior. It is simply the question; what is it about Christianity that makes it what it is?

The answer, clearly, revolves around Jesus. But I want to leave aside for now any thoughts about Jesus along the lines that 'he is God'. (That is more about 'who is Jesus?' than 'who was Jesus?') Also, we might leave aside those images of Jesus that bear little resemblance to the actual person who walked the earth. I am thinking, for instance, of how he is portrayed in pictures of the 'Sacred Heart'.

## The historical figure

Rather, think about the historical figure. Jesus was a Jew who lived in the Near East (present day Israel) 2,000 years ago. Current scholarship suggests that he lived between about 6 BC and about 30 AD. Christianity is focused on his person – more specifically, on what came out of his life and death. It hinges on what others made of him and saw in him.

Scholarship helps us get as near to the actual historical figure as is still possible so many centuries later. The main sources we have are the four gospels, but they are not written as historical information. They are better described as 'testimony'. In them, faith-inspired perspectives are woven into a biographical portrait (or, rather, four different portraits).

So, what can we say about the historical figure, Jesus of Nazareth? A good place to start is one of the earliest descriptions, in the Acts of the Apostles, which says that 'he went about doing good' (10:38). He was somebody whose goodness was remarkable. And the goodness that flowed from him had a very significant effect on those who came into contact with him.

There were different facets to his goodness. He was what we

might call a wonder-worker. While not all the so-called miracles of the gospels may be historical records in our sense, there was certainly a strong core, especially of works of healing. This is something he was known for.

He was also what we might call a liberator. He brought inner freedom to many people. Meeting Jesus was for many an experience of acceptance and inclusion, of being brought in from the cold. It was an experience of rediscovering their own humanity and the joy of being a human being. Often, this occurred in the context of a meal – the so-called 'table-fellowship' that could well be called Jesus' 'signature activity'.

He was also a storyteller of great vision and imagination. His sayings and images and stories have become part of our language – 'salt of the earth', the 'pearl of great price', 'throwing the first stone', the 'good Samaritan', the 'widow's mite'. It is not just the imaginative power that attracts; it is the vision of life or philosophy of life contained in his sayings and stories.

## Compassion

'Compassion' is the word that perhaps best captures what runs through all these facets of his goodness. The word crops up in two of the gospels' most famous stories – the Good Samaritan (Luke 10:33) and the Prodigal Son (Luke 15:20). But it was more than just a key word in Jesus' storytelling. It was at the heart of his activity. He felt compassion for the widow of Nain (Luke 7:13), for the blind men (Matthew 20:34), for the leper (Mark 1:41). He looked on the crowds with compassion (Matthew 9:36).

Jesus' compassion was for what the gospels generically call 'the poor' – a term which includes, not just the economically deprived, but also the physically disabled, the marginalised, the sinner, the failure, those destitute in any way. And there is nothing 'soft' about the Greek word used in the texts. It has to do with one's innards, gut, viscera. Compassion means emotionally and spiritually entering right into the pain of another, so that their experience becomes one's own.

There is also a further source for his compassion, in his own prayer life and his sense of 'God'. The gospels show him as somebody with an intense spirituality or mysticism underlying his very practical and overflowing goodness. They also present this as quite original and distinctive. He prayed to God as Abba, an Aramaic term meaning something like 'my own dear father (as in the 'Our Father', Luke 11:2). He addressed God and spoke of God with a striking intimacy.

Here he was continuing in the long line of Jewish prophets such as Isaiah, Jeremiah and Ezekiel. All of their lives too were 'taken over' by their sense of God. But this is not to be taken in a narrowly 'religious' sense. Jesus' sense of God was an intense sense of God as being 'bent upon' humanity, as being passionately concerned that all God's people know the joy of being a human being. So, the sense of God and a care for God's people go hand in hand.

What was happening was that Jesus' prayer led him to 'feel the feelings of God' – God's own compassion. He experienced God's feelings for God's people being channelled through his being. But it was not only the feelings of intense love. It was also feelings of anger – God's 'wrath' – at everything in humanity's dealings with one another that was opposed to how human beings were meant to be.

*Kingdom of God*
Jesus himself had a term for all this, a distinctive term which he chose to communicate what he was about, what today we might call his logo. That term is usually translated as 'kingdom of God'. Kingdom is not a very serviceable word today, so other translations have been proposed, such as 'reign' of God or 'rule' of God.

Jesus' main message was his proclaiming that this rule of God is at hand (indeed these are his first words in Mark's gospel, 1:15). He proclaims it mainly by his actions, as described above. He proclaims it also in word, especially his stories and images. And the two dovetail. For example, his action of table fellowship with outsiders dovetails with his image of God's 'kingdom' as a banquet.

Jesus never defines what kingdom means. He alludes to it; 'the kingdom of heaven is like ...' Nobody will ever fully know what it meant for him. But we can say something about it. It is not about politics and power. It is about a state of affairs where

God's dream for humanity is being realised. As Jesus speaks of
it, he sees it as both here already and as still imminent. On the
one hand he says, 'the kingdom of God is among you' (Luke
17:21). On the other he teaches his disciples to pray, 'your kingdom come' (Luke 11:2).

His message here is not one of doom and judgement, but one
of joy and freedom. But it is not just a message; it is a presence.
In his presence people experience life as grace. People are
graced by his presence. Relationships of domination and exclus-
ion give way to relationships of grace. There is a graciousness to
everything; there is cause for gratitude. Humanity here is at its
best; which is the same as saying that God's Spirit is breaking
through.

*Religious?*
It is worth pausing here to ask the question; was Jesus religious?
The answer is not simple and could be 'no' as much as 'yes'.
First of all, he was not a priest of the Jewish religion. He was an
ordinary, undistinguished layman, marginal to the circles of
those who controlled things religious. So, while obviously a
spiritual person, he was not a religious figure.

Second, religion was not his core concern in the way that it
might be for the clergy of the religion. The passion of his heart
was twofold, both God and God's people. His passion was
about that point where 'God' and 'people' intersect. His energy
was around people having life and having it to the full (John
10:10) – which was also God's passion as he perceived and
experienced it. So these two run together; a strong humanitarian
passion and a deep divinely-inspired motivation.

Third, sometimes in the gospels he can appear to be almost
anti-religious. I mean this in the sense that he is presented as
being critical of the religion of his time. Think of his debates
with the religious figures over the Sabbath, where he stands up
for ordinary people against the demands of a religion that is too
stringent and legalistic. He is even seen accusing them of
putting their own traditions before the truths of God (Mark 7:9).

Or think of the story of the Pharisee and the Publican. It is
introduced as a parable he told 'to some who trusted in themselves that they were righteous and regarded others with contempt'

(Luke 18:9). Here the complacency and self-satisfaction of 'religious' people cause others, supposed 'sinners', to be dismissed and ostracised. In such ways religion is seen to be an obstacle to rather than a facilitator of God's people becoming more fully human.

But in all this, what Jesus ultimately wants is the transformation of religion, not its demise. He wants to get back to the heart of what religion is all about – which is what is in God's heart for God's people, what he meant by the 'kingdom' of God. In the peculiar way of human beings, the holders of religious power found this hard to grasp and hard to take.

*Who is he?*
His coming on the scene and the impact he made attracted a following. This could be described with the image of concentric circles. The inner circle was made up of a stable group of twelve specially-chosen companions. The number twelve was symbolic of the twelve tribes of Israel. It indicates that in his thinking he envisaged a transformation within his own Jewish religion. He visualised a renewed 'people of God'.

Another circle outside this was made up of other followers. Some are called disciples, others not, but all have experienced an attraction and a 'calling'. They include many long-term followers and people who also lent practical support for his itinerant mission. Mary and Martha, Zacchaeus, Lazarus, Mary of Magdala, Levi, Nathaniel are some of the names.

An outer circle was made up of what the gospels call 'the crowds'. Crowds followed or awaited him wherever he went. They were a fluid mixture, people coming and going, people on whom he had an enduring impact, people who came along and drifted away again, people we know little about, people who turned against him, people who were against him and then changed.

From amongst all these people and the experience they were having, the question begins to formulate itself: 'Who is he?' At one point Jesus is talking with his close companions about what people are saying about him: 'Who do people say that I am?' (Mark 8:27). Is he a prophet, or Elijah finally returned, or who? On another occasion, the crowds are asking: 'Who is this, that even the wind and the sea obey him?' (Mark 4:41). When he cures a blind and mute man, they ask: 'Can this be the Son of David?' (Matthew 12:23).

We have to leave aside inherited perspectives. People did not look at Jesus and see God. They saw a human person. But there was a growing sense among some who saw him that he was 'more than what you see', that he was 'more than any other'. A prophet – certainly. But more? Was he 'sent'? That, it seems, was the sequence in people's thinking about him.

It is clear, however, that this is not of his own prompting. The evidence indicates that he was not proclaiming himself. He was not in the business of making claims for himself, or setting himself up. Rather, he was pointing beyond himself. He was proclaiming God's kingdom – that was his focus. He was gripped by this, taken over by this, with little room for focus on himself.

At the same time, it is legitimate to ask how he saw himself. What did he know about himself? Who did he think he was? Answers here cannot fully satisfy. A big part of it is that the story is being written by people who have come to certain beliefs about who he was, as a result of what they call his resurrection. It is hard for us, reading the story, to separate historical fact from beliefs that are woven back into the account.

Granted that, there is something we can say. He did see himself as the latest in a long line of prophets. But he also saw himself as more than just the latest in that line. He came to realise that God's kingdom, which he proclaimed, was also bound up in some unique way with his own life and destiny. Only in that indirect sense was his focus on himself. (The parable of the landowner and the tenants at Matthew 21:33-41 could be taken to reflect this.)

Along with that, the prayer experience I spoke of above testifies to a characteristic self-consciousness on his part, a quite original sense of being present to God and of God being present to him. Self-consciousness here is different from self-knowledge. We can imagine a sense of self that is real, but inarticulate, gradually growing more explicit, becoming more articulate. But the designation of Jesus as 'Son of God' or 'Lord' is best regarded as arising out of the resurrection experience of his followers.

*Death and after*

Jesus' life was brought to a premature end when he was in his thirties. During his few intense years of public activity, resistance to him had been growing among the religious authorities. He was perceived as a threat, both because he was gaining the loyalty of many and because of his connecting acceptance of God's coming reign with a decision about himself.

The religious authorities presented this as being also a threat to political stability. Thereby they enlisted the co-operation of the occupying Roman power, which then tried, condemned and executed Jesus. Thus his premature death was also the death of an innocent victim of violence and prejudice. In his death, he becomes one with 'the poor', those for whom he had lived his life.

Jesus' arrest was facilitated by his betrayal by one of his twelve companions, Judas. But he was also denied by Peter, leading figure among his followers. And the remainder of his followers also deserted him out of fear. Given this scenario, what unfolded next was the last thing expected. What happened was a remarkable turnaround and regrouping on the part of his disciples. Some claimed that Jesus, risen from death, had appeared to them.

Before moving on to this, reflect on how different the present chapter would have been if we had started with the idea that 'God became man' or the idea that Jesus is 'the Son of God'. We would have missed the process whereby people first came to say such things. We might also have found ourselves left with a quite unreal picture of this historical figure.

It seems better to begin where real people like Peter began. They encountered him in person, as a person. They travelled with him, they were fascinated with him, they were changed by him. They invested their hopes in him – hopes that were then fulfilled in a most unexpected way. What makes Christianity what it is, is what came out of this.

*For Reflection*

Think about the picture (or different pictures) of Jesus you have had over the years. Compare that to the picture presented here.

CHAPTER FIVE

# *Good News*

The resurrection, said Saint Augustine, is 'the most distinctive point of the faith of Christians'.[2] It is the core, the heart, the centre, what makes Christianity what it is. Everything about the life of Jesus leads up to it. Without the resurrection his whole life comes to the same thing as anybody else's. With it, everybody else's life comes to the same thing as his. In this chapter and the next, we explore the meaning of the resurrection.

## *Good news*

But this is not always where the emphasis goes in people's sense of their Christian faith. There is, for instance, an inherited perception that Christianity is mainly about morality. Certainly in the Catholic Church, there has been a preoccupation with managing people's behaviour, especially in sexual matters. Such detailed control of behaviour gives the impression that Christianity's main concern is moral conformity.

Something huge has gone wrong here. How we live is obviously a big part of being a Christian, but there is more than behaviour at the heart of the Christian message. It would be more accurate to say that Christianity is a worldview than that it is a morality. It is a spiritual view of life with implications for living. The view of life comes first, the way of living follows. Christianity is about the meaning of life.

And if we look at the annual cycle of Christian ritual, again the emphasis seems to lie elsewhere. The feast of Christmas and the commemoration of Good Friday are the two big days, bigger than Easter in the consciousness of most Christians. Maybe it is understandable; after all, birth and to death are two of the experiences we are most responsive to. But it has also been remarked how Christians can appear to be more Good Friday people than Easter Sunday people, more gloomy than glowing!

When people first heard the Christian message they asked: 'What should we do?' The question was a response to the disciples' testimony that Jesus was risen (Acts 2:32-37). The 'embryo' from which Christianity grew is there. It lies in what happened to the original companions of Jesus. Their disappointment and betrayal and flight at his death was transformed into their re-grouping and witnessing. The core is his resurrection. They proclaim simply: 'He is risen'.

So, Christianity is an announcement, a proclamation. It is news. Like all news, the implications and ramifications will unfold gradually, with time and reflection. But the core is a new message. This is what is contained in the word 'gospel', which refers to the four texts that carry the original story. It is an old English word meaning 'good news' or 'good message'. The Greek word in the Bible – *eu-aggelion*, Latin *evangelium* – means the same.

The proclamation is that Jesus is risen, and the news is good. It is good, not so much in the sense of 'good-for-him', as when somebody recovers from an illness, but good-for-us. The announcement is good news for our lives and good news for our world. In fact, it is the best piece of good news that the world could hope to hear.

*What happened?*

To answer the question 'what happened?' we could say that, by some magic or miraculous act of divine intervention, God plucked Jesus out of the grave, brought him back to life, put him back together again. This, then, would be the greatest miracle, following on all the miracles Jesus performed during his life.

It would also be an easy answer. If the resurrection is to be believed, we are talking about something at the intersection of time and timelessness. That kind of thing is not easy to talk about. I would like to leave to one side the language of miracles and divine interventions, and talk in a different way about what happened.

Let us begin with the disciples and what happened them. There was, I have said, an astonishing turn-around. At the arrest of Jesus they fled. They were not there at his death. The next we hear of them is that they have come together again and are testifying, proclaiming that he has risen from the dead and appeared to them.

What happened? It has been said that the disciples were brought together by an act of forgiveness. This is very clear in the case of Peter. We are familiar with the story of his threefold denial of Jesus after Jesus was arrested. Next, at the end of John's gospel we read the conversation he has with the risen Jesus with his threefold avowal: 'Yes Lord, you know that I love you' (John 21:15-19).

There is a correspondence here. On the one hand we have the disciple's betrayal transcended with a reconciliation. On the other we have Jesus' death transcended by his rising. The disciples experienced a reconciliation and reconciliation is not one-sided. It was not some internally simulated experience. It corresponds with an external encounter, with Jesus' present among them.

The way they describe this encounter is a strange blend. On the one hand Jesus is a clearly physical presence. He eats with them, they can touch him and talk with him. On the other, he can just appear in a closed room and he can disappear in an instant from their sight. In relation to the person they were familiar with, there was continuity and there was discontinuity. He was recognisable and he was different.

That is why it is unsatisfactory to speak of it in terms of God bringing Jesus back to life. If he was brought back to life he would be the same as before (like Lazarus in John 11). We are talking about resurrection, not resuscitation. It was not that Jesus had come back to the same old life. Rather, Jesus had broken through to a new sphere of existence. It is this transformed existence which the disciples experience as his presence among them.

The Letter to the Hebrews offers the image of the anchor. 'We have this hope, a sure and steadfast anchor of the soul, a hope that enters the inner shrine behind the curtain, where Jesus, a forerunner on our behalf, has entered' (6:19-20). He 'has entered' into or broken through into this sphere of transformed existence and he is present to us from there.

We might speak of it as a heightened activity of God's Spirit. We have already spoken of God's being universally present in the world. We can see how God was powerfully present in the life of Jesus. Now in his death we are seeing that presence reaching its point of greatest intensity. In the words of Paul, Jesus became 'a life-giving spirit' (1 Corinthians 15:45).

*The question*

Next, we can inquire into the meaning of what happened. I will take this in two stages. In the next chapter, I will discuss what it says about who Jesus is and what the disciples come to say about him. Here I want to discuss what it says about ourselves and the life we live. I will be talking about the light which the resurrection throws on our questions about life.

This brings us back to the discussion of faith, of the different beliefs people have about the meaning of life. There are different beliefs because there are different interpretations, and there are different interpretations because the evidence in life is ambiguous, capable of being read in more than one way. Belief in Jesus' resurrection speaks into this situation and offers light.

Recall what was said about the conflicting evidence. There is the goodness of life; the joy, the love, the sense of 'more', the sense of security. And there is the darkness; the cruelty and misery, how we can feel trapped and grow cynical. The wicked prosper while the innocent suffer; and senseless suffering has visited countless millions. Yet regularly people transcend their circumstances and bring something that is nothing less than amazing out of the pain and the injustice.

The ambiguity extends to God. There is a passage in the Bible where God is about to destroy the people in the desert because of their infidelity. Moses remonstrates with God; what will the Egyptians think of you if, having freed this people, you now destroy them? It is as if Moses is getting God to 'count to ten', so as not to fly off the handle. And God relents (Numbers, chapter 14).

The story is not really about a capricious, unpredictable God. It is more about a struggle going on in people's heads about the true face of God. For the Old Testament people, the evidence was ambiguous. At one time, God is experienced as tender, compassionate, utterly faithful. At another, God is distant, fearful, indifferent. The unresolved sense of God stands out in the same incident:

> The Lord is slow to anger and abounding in steadfast love,
> forgiving iniquity and transgression,
> but by no means clearing the guilty,
> visiting the iniquity of the parents upon the children
> to the third and the fourth generation (Numbers 14:18).

CHAPTER FIVE                                                   39

We have here a series of questions that in the end cannot be answered from within our experience. We have a question about life and its ambiguities. We have a question about God and the ambiguities surrounding God. Perhaps also we have a question about ourselves, who we are and what we are; matter or spirit, saint or sinner, grace or sin?

*An answering movement*

All of this 'hangs on the cross', as it were, the weight of these questions. For Christians these questions come to their climax in Jesus. His own living represents a definite stance about both the question of life's meaning and about the question of God's identity. But his humiliating death strongly suggests that his hope around these two was in vain.

His living was itself a statement about life's meaning. It said that life's meaning lies in the power of compassion and forgiveness and justice to transform hearts and relationships and society. And his living was a statement about God. It said that passion and compassion are the true face of God; that God truly is hope for the poor, future for the sinner; that God is at work in the world for our eternal enchantment.

Yet death on the cross places Jesus alongside all the poor and abandoned of the world, all who have suffered innocently, all the forgotten and forlorn. It is not just that Jesus and his life-vision are on trial on the cross, but also his God is on trial. If Jesus' vision dies, then his God dies with him. Looking on at Jesus' crucifixion, we might well ask about his God: 'Is this not the God who stands aloof – if indeed God exists at all?'

Seen in this framework, Jesus' resurrection has for Christians the quality of an answering movement 'from behind the curtain'. The resurrection is the raising up and affirmation of all that Jesus stood for. His life's vision, his life's work, are embraced by God. His life's trust or 'faith', is taken into God's own heart.

But there is more to God's embracing Jesus in death. Christians understand that God also takes to God's self all who have died 'alongside' Jesus – innocent, poor, abandoned, forsaken, condemned. In fact, all deaths are caught up in his death. All destinies are locked into his rising. Resurrection is about the ultimate future of all God's beloved. It is the confirmation of what we had dared hope, the revelation that the future of all is a future as God's beloved.

This means that Jesus' resurrection reveals what our human destiny is. It unveils the ultimate shape of things. The pattern of human existence is a pattern of transformation, patterned on his living and dying and rising. Life is about breaking through in the power of God's Spirit to the new sphere of existence. And this is 'good news' – in relation to the ambiguities about life, in relation to the question about God, in relation to the questions we have about our own selves.

### Already

In a sense life goes on as before. The tensions and contradictions and confusions are still there. Nothing is ever resolved this side of the grave. But in another sense everything is different, everything is suffused by his presence. Jesus comes to us from our future, from where he has gone 'on our behalf'. In a very real way the future is already.

This echoes how Jesus himself spoke about the 'kingdom of God' and God's dream for humanity. Its realisation is still outstanding; and yet it is here. With the perspective of resurrection we can speak with a new confidence about the grace that is life. We can embrace with a new confidence our trust about life, our instinct to hope in life's worthwhileness. We have that 'anchor of the soul'. His rising from the dead into that further sphere, into God, anchors our deepest hope. We live from where he is.

### For reflection

Think back to the opening quote from Augustine, that the resurrection is 'the most distinctive point of the faith of Christians'. How would you relate that to your own faith?

CHAPTER SIX

# *The God-side of Jesus*

The resurrection is 'good news' about the meaning of life. But it also draws us into the identity of Jesus himself; it is the full unfolding of who he is. We reflect here on how the resurrection opened up to people his 'God-side', or the roots of his identity in the divine.

This brings us to the central Christian doctrines of the Trinity and the Incarnation, topics deserving of extensive elaboration in their own right. But all we are looking for now is a sense of how these beliefs arose out of the experience of the resurrection, and an indication of their basic content.

### Following Jesus

During the short years of his public life, Jesus gathered a following. Some of these were people whom he called to follow him. But it was 'follow' in a peculiar sense, compared to other teachers and wise people who had their devotees. Like them, he attracted people to subscribe to his teachings, his message, his vision. But unlike them, there was also a personal allegiance. In his case it was 'follow me'.

This already anticipates the situation after the resurrection. Before his death, while Jesus invited this personal following, his own focus was on his message rather than on himself. His focus was the kingdom of God. Only with the experience of his resurrection did the focus shift decisively to his own person. In a famous phrase, the proclaimer became the proclaimed. He proclaimed God's kingdom; now people proclaim him.

Think of great figures in the tradition of Christianity, such as Francis of Assisi from the Middle Ages, or Mother Teresa from the last century. They too built up a following. But they did not say 'follow me'. They did not call people to a personal loyalty to themselves. Rather, they invited people to follow Christ. It is the difference between subscribing to a person's vision, and the more personal 'following' where this person becomes the focus of loyalty.

It is a key issue in our time. Today, people can readily see in

Jesus an exemplary human being. The description in the Acts of the Apostles – 'he went about doing good' – is compelling and extremely attractive. This is everything human beings are meant to be. But it is a big step from admiration to allegiance, from high regard to personal devotion.

There is a kind of generation gap here. Older generations of Christians put a great emphasis on divinity in Jesus. Many would be happy with the stark statement: 'Jesus is God'. They would have, corresponding to this, a weaker sense of Jesus' humanity. For instance, if asked to explain the gospel incident of Jesus walking on the water many would respond: 'Well, he was God after all.'

Younger generations, in contrast, are at ease with Jesus as a human person and, indeed, as an inspirational and challenging figure. Their difficulty would be in getting to grips with Jesus' divinity. Yet this is what the resurrection invites us to do. It invites us to move beyond being captivated with his humanity, without losing our appreciation of it. It invites us to look deeper into his humanity and to find that it also embodies divinity.

*From experience to reflection*
The resurrection experience generated reflection on what I am calling the 'God-side' of Jesus. But in order to appreciate the dynamic we need to take off what somebody called 'our fifth-century spectacles'. This refers to the period into the fourth century AD when the major doctrines concerning Jesus (Trinity and Incarnation) were defined, after centuries of debate and refinement.

For Christians ever since, these doctrines have been the 'lens' through which we interpret earlier times. So, when we go to read about Jesus in the New Testament, we are already thinking 'Divine' and 'Second Person of the Trinity'. But these categories were not available to the people of the time. This is what makes it difficult for us to appreciate how things actually evolved.

Think of the sequence of events for somebody like Peter. First, he encountered a human being, Jesus of Nazareth, who appeared like any other. Next, he became attracted, captivated, committed; to the point where he is reported as saying: 'Lord, to whom can we go? You have the words of eternal life' (John 6:68). He came to see Jesus as 'more than any other'. He came to sense that something of God is present here in a remarkable, extraordinary way.

So, on one side, Jesus' own sense of himself was moving towards of seeing himself as bound up in a decisive way with God's action in the world. On the other side, the disciples' sense of him had been edging in this direction also. The resurrection was for them a confirmation of this. They come to see him explicitly as the decisive event in God's interaction with God's people. Designations such as 'Lord' and 'Son of God' will flow from this.

John's account of the Last Supper has Jesus saying to his companions: 'Whoever has seen me has seen the Father' (John 14:9). The phrase captures quite well where people like Peter arrived at in reflecting on their resurrection experience. It may well have been included in the gospel story from that perspective. They came to say that, in encountering Jesus, they were encountering God.

The language is not cerebral, but experiential. And the experience is articulated, not in theoretical, but in symbolic terms – as in the symbols 'Father' and 'Son' above. Such terms seek to convey an experience; that Jesus is to God as son is to father. They are that close. Likewise other terms used of Jesus, such as 'Lord', or 'Word' of God. They articulate that Jesus, in his humanity, is more of God than of the earth.

The experience generates another key symbol also, namely, 'Spirit'. To the Romans Paul says:

> If the Spirit of him who raised Jesus from the dead dwells in you, he who raised Christ from the dead will give life to your mortal bodies also, through his Spirit that dwells in you (8:11).

And he ends his second letter to Corinth: 'The grace of the Lord Jesus Christ, the love of God, and the communion of the Holy Spirit be with all of you.'

So, at this early stage, a three-fold way of talking about God has developed out of the experience – Father, Son, Spirit. But note how the language includes us. It is not about a God out there, but one who 'dwells in you'. The letter to the Romans continues: 'you have received a spirit of adoption. When we cry

"Abba! Father!" it is that very Spirit bearing witness with our spirit that we are children of God, and if children, then heirs with Christ' (8:15-17).

We are part of the picture. The resurrection is experienced as the outpouring of the Spirit, who incorporates us into God. Paul's image is adoption; we are genuinely part of God's 'family' but in a way distinct from Jesus as 'son'. John's image is the more radical one of a new birth: 'no one can enter the kingdom of God without being born of water and Spirit ... You must be born from above' (John 3:5-7).

### Experience, symbol, doctrine

So, reflection on the resurrection leads to talking about Jesus as part of a three-fold self-manifestation of God. Inseparable from this is that the believers see themselves as incorporated into the mystery of God. When Christians talk about God, they are also and unavoidably talking about themselves; and not just themselves, but all humanity.

At the same time, big questions arise. Is Jesus divine or human? How could he be both? If he is divine, are there now two gods? Does 'Spirit' mean that there are three? It took Christians centuries to come to sort out these issues, well into the fourth century. What we call 'heresies' are the formulations along the way that were deemed unsatisfactory – for instance, that Jesus was not really human, just God 'dressed up' in a human costume.

The main definitions (or 'doctrines') in question are those of the Incarnation (humanity and divinity in Jesus) and the Trinity (God as both three and one). But the important thing here is to note the process or sequence in what unfolded. First, the experience – of Jesus' life, death and transformed, risen presence. Second, the symbols that articulate this – for instance: 'Son of God'. Third, the doctrines – in answer to the questions that arose, demanding theoretical reflection and definition.

But the doctrines are not the experience! They are more like parameters or boundaries around what we can and cannot say in fidelity to the experience. So, for instance, we cannot say that there are three Gods. We have to say that there is one God who is both Father, Son and Spirit. We cannot say that Jesus is only apparently human, or only half-God. We have to say that he is fully human and fully divine.

There is a real danger of truncation. Imagine the experience as the base of a pyramid, then the images and symbols for the experience, then the doctrines at the apex. When we look through our 'fifth century spectacles', we may see the apex only. Then we are left with dry, lifeless theoretical formulations, severed from the experiences that motivated them. We have the fifth century formula without the first century experience.

The big questions came after. First there were the people who had the experience and made the confession of faith, as eloquently as they could. It would be better for us to start there. We are better starting, not with the fifth century dogma, but by entering into the experience of people like Peter and John and Paul. They did not have the theoretical language, terms like 'Trinity' and 'Incarnation'. But they knew the meaning, because they had the experience.

If we enter into their experience of Jesus, it might bring us to the point of feeling with them the truth of the words: 'Whoever has seen me has seen the Father'. We would appreciate with them that 'in him all the fullness of God was pleased to dwell' (Colossians 1:19). That would be more valuable than being able to talk learnedly about how God could be both three and one, or how Jesus could be both human and divine.

*Trinity*

Let us elaborate a little more on what is meant by Trinity. It should now be clear that it is not abstract speculation about God. Rather, the original Christians found themselves speaking in trinitarian terms as they reflected on the God they experienced in Jesus Christ. The language grew organically from the experience.

The simplest expression of the experience is probably that of the first letter of John (4:16): 'God is love'. This is far more than saying that God is very nice. It means that in Jesus we have encountered the true face of God. The true face of God, as manifest in Jesus' life, is pure love for humanity, utter passion for humanity, unfathomable desire that people experience fullness of humanity – which is the complete joy of being children of God.

That is 'love' from our side. From God's side, it means, in a contemporary expression, that God is community. God is not, as traditionally imagined, an isolated, remote 'old-man-in-the-sky'. God's own self is the perfect actualisation of love. That is what the language of 'Father, Son and Spirit' is pointing to. God's 'inner life' is a dynamic interaction, the eternal realisation of love. This leads to speaking of God as a community of being.

The love that is God overflows itself, in the creation of the evolving universe, and in the imagining and creating of humanity in particular. This overflowing reaches its full expression in what Christians call the Incarnation – the 'becoming flesh' – where divinity and humanity are one in Jesus.

In a further moment, the life, death and resurrection of Jesus becomes the experience of 'Spirit'. Spirit is the abiding presence of God in the world. This abiding presence is a power drawing all humanity into the divine-human unity. But also, it is what has been there since the dawn of humanity. The presence of 'Spirit', experienced and celebrated in so many different religious traditions, is now come to its full articulation and expression.

So, 'Trinity' is not a bland 'three equals one'. It is more profound and more personal. It is an insight into who God is, the eternal mystery of love. 'God' is a name to denote something we do not understand. But Trinity puts a face to the name; it is the 'who' behind the name. 'God' would remain just a name except that God has opened up to humanity, in a trusting and vulnerable unveiling of God's own self.

There are not two Gods, the God of God's inner life and the God down here. The one who exists as eternal mystery of love is the one who has come indescribably close to humanity in Jesus and who remains close as Spirit. This is to say that, in Jesus and in the continuing experience of the Spirit, we are in touch, not with intermediaries, but with the very self of God. This is not a communication from God, but a communication of God, in which we become part of God.

*Humanity and divinity*
To talk about Jesus is to talk about God. That is the thrust of this chapter. And talking about God is inseparable from talking about ourselves. When we talk about God, we ourselves are part of what we are talking about. We are part of what God wants to

be. This in turn profoundly affects our ideas of humanity and divinity.

When we speak of Jesus as both human and divine, there is lurking in the background our tendency to keep human and divine quite separate. We tend to see them as two different things entirely. We allow one exception; the only place where the two meet is in Jesus. This sets us on the wrong track immediately.

In contrast, I recall how Mahatma Gandhi used this language when writing somewhere about non-violence. He said that, to do nothing in the face of violence is 'to surrender your humanity'. To resist with violence at least shows concern; it is 'to enter into your humanity'. But to respond non-violently is to use the weapons of God and 'to enter into your divinity'.

He is talking about our divinity. We are more than 'just' human beings. We are spiritual beings and there are depths to our humanity. Our becoming more fully human is, in fact, a process of entering into our divinity. As the Bible puts it, we are 'in the image of God' (Genesis 1:27).

Next, let us see how this links in with the disciples' experience of Jesus as Lord, as Word become flesh. The Irish theologian Enda Lyons wrote a book with the striking title, *Jesus: Self-Portrait by God*.[3] The book sees Jesus as God's perfect self-expression in human terms. Nothing has been lost in translation. This is the disciples' experience. In his humanity, Jesus is experienced as the perfect self-expression of divinity.

But this is only part of the picture. It is only complete when we see how the unity of humanity and divinity involves ourselves. Thus Meister Eckhart, a medieval Dominican mystic, spoke of a two-fold Incarnation. There is the historical Incarnation in time, that takes place in Jesus. And there is a mystical Incarnation in each one of us, when the Word is made flesh in us, when Jesus is born in our soul through faith – and we are born into God.

So humanity and divinity belong together. They are uniquely one in Jesus, but only so that they would be one in us. And so the early church spoke of Christian living as a process of 'divinisation', a matter of becoming divine. Our becoming more human, our becoming more Christian, is one single process of our entering into our divinity. We share humanity with Jesus so as to share divinity also, as sons and daughters with him in God.

Here again, we see how resurrection for Christians discloses the meaning of our human destiny. Reflection on our ordinary human experience would tell us that life is about becoming more human and resisting all that is anti-human. In resurrection perspective, this is seen in its fuller context. It is God's Spirit drawing us into our divinity, into God's trinitarian life.

*For reflection*
Reflect on the following: thinking about the 'God-side' of Jesus puts us in touch with the 'God-side' of ourselves. As a help, you could look up Andrei Rublev's famous fifteenth century icon of the Trinity.

CHAPTER SEVEN

# *Christian Faith*

Christian faith is the topic of this whole book; but the focus here is more specific. Here I am asking, not so much: 'What do Christian believe?', but rather: 'What kind of faith is it that Christians have?' The question links in with the earlier chapter on faith.

Christian faith is not the only kind of faith. Faith and believing characterise all human living. Because believing is part of being human, it manifests itself in a rich variety of ways. It is reflected in the variety of different religions, in different spiritualities, in ways that do not appear to be 'religious' at all. There may be no mention of God; there may even be a sense of there being no God; and yet there can be a lively sense of believing.

Nor is Christian faith the most basic kind of faith. The most basic faith is that 'thrust towards trust' that arises from deep within as well as from our interactions with life. Christian faith is something further. It is secondary in this sense. Understanding Christian faith is about situating it in relation to our ordinary everyday faith.

## A Dialogue

The way I picture it is to think of somebody who already has a 'faith-life'. People are not coming from nowhere. Unfortunately, 'nowhere' is how some people see those who do not profess Christian faith. People are coming from somewhere. And Christian faith is the outcome, or possible outcome, of their encounter with Christianity.

People have their personal experience of believing and Christianity is not meant to replace that prior faith. Unfortunately is has often been like that. Often it has been the case that 'mission' and missionaries suppress or paint over what was already there. But it is meant to be other than that. Christian faith is more like an enrichment, an expansion – a further step along the path.

I am thinking in terms of a dialogue, between the person of faith and Christianity, out of which comes a new faith-integration in that person. But if it is dialogue, then it is a two-way conversation. Christianity will speak into the faith that is already there, with its perspectives, with an invitation to transformation. Equally, the faith already alive will speak into Christianity, seeing angles to it, questioning it.

One aspect of it is about the expectations a person of faith brings to the dialogue with Christianity. For ordinary human faith sooner or later finds itself faced with questions it cannot answer from its own resources. For all its intuitive convictions about life's meaning, it does not know if its 'thrust to trust' is ultimately vindicated. It knows that it has no confirmation as to the 'ultimate shape of things'.

Most sharply, it feels vulnerable before the 'big questions' – what sense in suffering; the other side of death; the power of evil; forgiveness in guilt; the true face of God. So the person of faith comes to Christianity in an incomplete state. But all of this is also a yardstick by which to appraise Christianity. What does it have to offer on these fronts? A prior faith-life means that a person can dialogue with Christianity in a critical, searching spirit.

This idea of dialogue is relevant today. In the past people had Christian faith for longer than they could remember. And there was no other kind of faith. Today more and more people, even if they are baptised, come to adulthood with very little history of relating to Christianity. But, by and large, they do come to adult life with some history of engaging with life's experiences – which is also their 'faith' story.

*A Person*

So, what does the person of faith encounter when they encounter Christianity? The answer, quite simply, is a person. They do not encounter, first and foremost, a system of beliefs, nor a code of behaviour, nor a set of ritual practices. These are all subsequent, derivative. First there is a personal interaction, an encounter and relationship with the risen Jesus Christ.

I recall a sketch of a tele-evangelist, looking straight into the camera, straight into the viewer's eyes, and asking with supreme, solemn gravity: 'Have you accepted Jesus Christ as your personal Lord and Saviour?' This is one image, a caricature of the encounter, as a highly emotional 'jumping into the arms of Jesus'. It stands in sharp contrast to that other picture of Christianity, as a very dry, cerebral assent to doctrinal formulations.

A truer account would see the encounter operating at different levels. As somebody put it, Christian faith is a matter of the head and the heart and the hands – of mind, of feeling and of action (though the three can only be artificially separated). But the heart comes first, as we would expect when speaking of faith as a personal encounter.

Indeed, in scripture, the word faith is primarily about a sense of trust. Faith is a heart-word. For instance, when the Psalms picture God as a rock, a stronghold, a fortress; faith is about One who can be relied upon, who is worthy of huge trust. So Christian faith is the kind of trust that grows within a relationship to Jesus that is intimate and true. This is where we speak of the 'leap of faith', but it is a leap which echoes with our experience of human relationships.

Then there are the hands. The trust-engendering encounter that is the heart of Christian faith sets living in a new key. Faith is now reflected or expressed in how we live. It becomes visible in our living and lifestyle, in our behaviour and values, in the quality of our relationships. Thus we speak of following Christ, or discipleship. Here we see the commitment aspect of faith that we spoke of in the earlier chapter.

And faith is also in the head, the rational side of it. We work things out on the basis of our encounter. We work things out about who Jesus is and who God is. We work things out about the world we live in, about the big questions such as death and guilt, evil and suffering. Here, faith is our worldview, the knowledge born of trust. Calling it 'doctrines' or 'dogmas' hardly does it justice. Speaking, as Christians do, of a 'creed' comes closer.

There is an important distinction in all this between what we believe and who we believe. 'What' we believe is the creed, as well as the doctrines that are further elaborations of what we believe. But the heart of Christian faith is the 'who', the person of Jesus Christ and the believer's relationship to him.

*Personal but not Private*

Before continuing, a clarification is needed. The picture emerging could suggest something quite private. It could suggest a single individual somehow, somewhere, 'encountering Jesus' and ending up with Christian faith. As it stands, it is too private, in that it veers towards something too subjective, possibly even fanciful or deluded. It could imply that Christian faith is whatever somebody wants to make it into themselves.

I see the encounter in question as less direct, more mediated (that is, involving intermediaries), while remaining intensely personal. We are, after all, talking about a figure in history, two thousand years ago, with all the attendant difficulty of accessing who the real figure was. And we are talking about this figure as one with a huge 'presence' in the here and now, visible as he is in the faith of those who believe in him.

In other words, people come to Jesus by way of introductions. They come to Jesus through others and the encounter-experience that those others are having. In particular I am thinking of the community of those who believe – the ones who gather together for the Eucharistic meal and to listen to the words of scripture. Those words in turn introduce them to Jesus through the encounter-experience of the original disciples.

So the encounter is also a process of being initiated into a Christian community. It is not an isolated event, like Paul on the road to Damascus. It takes shape gradually, as a person engages with and enters into a community of believers. But more of this in the next chapter.

*What happens?*

I use the phrase 'a process of being initiated', because 'encounter' might imply a single occasion or event. Christian faith does not all happen in one blinding flash. It happens over time, it unfolds or opens out gradually. It is something ongoing. What I am talking about now is the overall shape of this ongoing encounter.

The encounter with Jesus is essentially the same as that of the original disciples. Apart from differences of detail and circumstance, what else would it be? Thus it is along the lines of what has been sketched already, where we looked at the historical figure of Jesus, what he was about, the effect he had on people, and the effect of his death and subsequent events on how they perceived him.

So, the encounter is about coming to a sense of who he is – the compassion, the passion. But it is far more than observing it from afar. Rather, it is about feeling what the characters of the gospel felt. It is about connecting with the life-giving spirit that flowed through him and from him. It is about experiencing in ourselves the transformation it wrought in people's hearts and lives. Much, perhaps most of this, is given to us through others around us, their spirit and faith and passion.

And the encounter is about what is further sensed within this. It is about the sense that God is with him, in him, more than God was ever with and in a person. It is about how this is brought to light in the resurrection experience. The encounter is about a realisation that God's Spirit fills him to such an extent that he becomes everything. 'He who has seen me has seen the Father.' 'In him all the fullness of God was pleased to dwell.'

Next, the encounter is about what we come to see in this about ourselves and our destiny, which is also the destiny of all, our life's project of being born into God. And the encounter is, finally, about the effect on our living – how our living, like that of the disciples, comes to be the expression of the hope that is within us.

The effect of this on a person's prior faith is in the nature of an affirmation or confirmation. The Letter to the Hebrews speaks of faith as 'the assurance of things hoped for, the conviction of things not seen' (11:1). The encounter brings ordinary faith to that further level of substantiation, assurance, conviction. It is like an answering movement from beyond. It confirms all the moving of God's Spirit that we had sensed in the undulating voyage of our life, as well as throughout humanity's history.

*A new creation*
So, what changes when, through encounter with Jesus, ordinary everyday faith is 'upgraded' to faith in him? In one sense all is changed; in another very little. Life itself, with all its perplexities, continues as before. The rich get richer; the innocent suffer; death terrifies; the power of sin is unabated. We ourselves do

not just jump out of doubt into certainty. It is still 'faith' and the questions do not just disappear.

And the person who has moved to Christian faith does not necessarily live differently than before. As will be discussed in a later chapter, people do not need Christianity to figure out how best to live as human beings. Nor is Christianity the only source of divine strength for the effort. For, as was said, that grace or Spirit is already there for us and in us, simply by virtue of our existence as human beings.

It is more that life is lived in a new key, a new tenor, a new context. It is the same life as ever, with the same questions and struggles and challenges. But it is experienced differently. It is like when a person is in love; so much goes on as before, but everything feels different. Is this the kind of thing Paul meant when saying: 'From now on, we regard no one from a human point of view ... if anyone is in Christ there is a new creation' (2 Corinthians 5:16-17).

What is concretely different might well be prayer. When two are in love, the obvious new element in their lives is the time they spend together. When faith becomes Christian, the new element is the togetherness. There is the time given specifically to the relationship; just being with (what Christians call contemplation), as well as getting to know (what they call meditation), and linking all that to life.

It goes deeper. We talk of how in marriage 'the two become one flesh'. In the encounter with Jesus, the relationship with him, there is a marrying, a becoming one. A single life-force, God's creative Spirit, animates both. Paul says: 'It is no longer I who live, but it is Christ who lives in me' (Galatians 2:20). It is a kind of consummation or coming-to-full-realisation of the Spirit-energy already flowing through ourselves and all God's creatures.

*For reflection*
Christian faith is about the heart, the hands and the head. Which of the three do you relate most strongly too? Which do you relate to weakly?

CHAPTER EIGHT

# *What is Church?*

Christian faith is about an encounter with Jesus Christ. But the encounter happens in the context of a community of faith. I alluded to this in the last chapter; now I wish to fill it out. And filling it out takes us into a reflection on church and what church is all about

The word 'church' provokes different reactions. Does it practise what it preaches? Is it more an impersonal institution than a spirit-filled community? Does authoritarian teaching override freedom? Is there one true church? Some of these issues will be taken up later. Here I wish to talk about what the church is meant to be.

*Difficulties*
Let me begin with two difficulties about the idea of church. First, people now distinguish between 'spirituality' and 'religion'. Organised religion is felt to be in decline in this part of the world. Spirituality is seen to be flourishing in many forms independent of religion. In all of this a distance has been created between spirituality and community.

In a celebrated phrase, ours is a time of 'believing without belonging'.[4] In disengaging from organised religion, many have remained connected with their own spiritual search. But they have disengaged from community. Spirituality today is often (but not always) a private affair of the individual. Sometimes it appears to be like another consumer product: I take what I like and bring it home. It is spirituality 'for me'.

In the same vein people can want Christianity without church. People sometimes say: 'Why do I need to confess to a priest? Can I not just talk to God in my own way.' Or: 'I get more from meditating watching a sunset than from going to Mass.' Many who would call themselves Christians feel that church is surplus to requirements for making spiritual progress.

The other difficulty is the suspicion that church might be, not just irrelevant, but even harmful to people's spiritual lives. There is huge disillusion today with church and religion. There are different reasons for this. But it is due in part, perhaps in no small part, to religion's own shortcomings.

There has even been some acknowledgment of this on the part of organised religion. For instance, a well-known Catholic Church document identified different reasons for the increase in atheism in the world. As part of this it said:

> Believers themselves often share some responsibility. Atheism springs from various causes, among which must be included a critical reaction against religion. Believers can thus have more than a little to do with the rise of atheism … they may conceal rather than reveal the true nature of God and of religion.[5]

What goes on in the church may seem like a million miles from the gospel. Religion can take on the very forms that Jesus is presented as castigating in the gospels. It can be constraining rather than liberating, suffocating the spirit. One person offered the image of a pot-bound plant for what church can be like today. It becomes caught up in itself, choking itself, starved of air.

Is there something in us that rebels against church, against organised religion? And if not, should there be? Maybe church can never measure up to what Jesus was about. At the same time, is there not something vital in the idea of church, even if so many actual instances of church fall short of the mark?

*A pattern*

In some important ways, church and religion follow the pattern of other organisations in history, a cycle of growth and stagnation and revival. First there is the charismatic figure, prophetic and inspirational, revealing hidden depths and possibilities, revealing people to themselves. This figure attracts a following, an inspired community, rooted in him and with a strong outward or missionary thrust.

After a time, understandably, attention turns to organisation. In the case of Christianity, when the original followers were dying out and there was no longer a direct link to the founder, a concern emerged for fidelity and continuity. In the last writings of the New Testament Christians are beginning to talk about issues of orthodoxy and of leadership.

With this, inevitably, some of the focus turns inwards This is intended to be self-strengthening but it can become instead a focus on self-preservation and self-perpetuation. There is then a shift from proclaiming Christ to promoting church. When this happens, the means to the end itself becomes the end. And with this turn inward comes a preoccupation with power and control and centralisation.

There is a process of institutionalisation that brings with it an ever weaker connection to the originating vision. It ends up in what has been called a culture of complacency. There is a lot of self-satisfaction and much less sense of being challenged (or wanting to be challenged) by the vision. Narrow functional goals are directed to maintaining the *status quo*. There is little interest in external feedback or loyal internal critique. Decline and decay set in.

The choice, then, is either more decay by maintaining the *status quo* or a revitalisation inspired by the original vision and mission. The history of the church can be seen as the story of the tension between the two, the institutional tendency and the charismatic energy. If, at a given time, all people can see is the institution and the decay, that does not mean that there is nothing else to see, nothing more to what church can be.

*Church*
So, originally, what is church? One caricature portrays it as Jesus calling aside his main followers (called apostles), giving them detailed instructions about the 'church' he intends to set up, and how it is to be run, and then 'ordaining' them as its first bishops. The trouble with this caricature can be seen if we ask: What if Jesus had died, full stop?

Church only makes sense if Jesus is risen. It is an outcome of the resurrection, a response to resurrection. This is reflected in the tradition of seeing the feast of Pentecost as the birthday of the church. We can still say that church originates in Jesus, but it only comes to birth as a result of his resurrection.

The word used for church in the New Testament is *ekklesia*. But the word does not yet have the connotations of our ecclesiastical structure and institution. The Greek word means a gathering of people, an assembly. In the New Testament it means specifically the gathering of Christians for the 'breaking of bread', as the Eucharist was first known.

It was gathering on an intimate, human-sized scale. Typically it took place in somebody's house. So, for example, Paul in his letters greets Nympha and 'the church in her house', or Philemon and 'the church in your house', or Prisca and Aquila and 'the church in their house' (Colossians 4:15; Philemon 2; Romans 16:3-5).

Less frequently, church refers to the body of disciples at large (e.g. Ephesians 5:25: 'Christ loved the church'). But its usual meaning is this church or that church, not in the sense of a building (they had no churches in that sense) but in the sense of a gathering that was small and local.

A good translation of *ekklesia* would be 'convocation'. Significantly, this comprises the two words with (con) and calling (vocation). So church means people who gather because they are called, that is, drawn or attracted in some way. But it also means that the calling is communal, a 'together' experience. To be a Christian is not just to be called individually. It is about being gathered together.

At the core of this gathering is Jesus' instruction, at his last Supper meal: 'Do this in memory of me.' As Christians follow this instruction, by gathering for the 'together-act' of the breaking of bread, they know his presence. He who has broken through death by the power of God's Spirit; as Luke puts it, they recognise him in the breaking of bread (Luke 24: 31, 35).

This presence is also the communication of his Spirit to them. Then, in the power of the Spirit, they carry on his mission. So his presence is real in two ways; in the gathering for the breaking of bread, and in the way of living that it inspires. Thus the church is described in the Acts of the Apostles (2: 42, 44-45):

> They devoted themselves to the apostles' teaching and fellowship, to the breaking of bread and the prayers ...
> All who believed were together and had all things in common; they would sell their possessions and goods and distribute the proceeds to all, as any had need.

*Mission*
From this I would take two words around which to express what church means – the words mission and community. Being

a Christian is about being together as Christians and being sent as Christians. Church is a community called together around Christ and focused on mission.

First the word mission. Here we need to forget the 'foreign missions' and the 'parish mission'. The thing to grasp is that mission is not primarily something that the church engages in. Originally mission is about God. It originates in God, it is an activity of God. And then it is something that the church is caught up in or, more accurately, born from.

The gospel of John brings this out clearly. A characteristic of that gospel is that the language of sending is pervasive. As a prelude there is John the Baptist: 'Sent by God' (1:6). He points to Jesus, who repeatedly and persistently speaks of 'the one who sent me' (e.g. 5:30; 6:38; 8:29; 12:44-45). Jesus is presented to us as the one sent by the Father. He is God's outreach to humanity, sent to achieve God's purpose of communicating 'life' to God's people (10:10).

As Jesus' own life nears its conclusion, he points us to the Spirit 'whom the Father will send in my name' (14:26); or, 'whom I will send to you from the Father' (15:26). The Spirit is to continue Jesus' mission to us. The Spirit is the permanent presence of God's outreach among us.

Finally, the disciples' experience of Jesus risen is an experience of being sent. 'As the Father sent me, so I send you' (20:21). The movement towards humanity that originated in God continues in us, in the power of the Spirit. To be a disciple is to continue Jesus' mission.

This gives church its identity. It is the community of disciples who are caught up in the divine outreach. Church is born out of God's mission and has no meaning apart from it. It is not 'church then mission', but 'mission then church'. First, God's outreach; then church as a partner in God's activity. When church loses this focus, the mission may become church-centred instead of God-centred, about self-preservation and self-aggrandisement.

## Community

Second, church is community. As originally conceived, to be a Christian is to belong. It is to be one of those who gather. It is to be part of a togetherness, a fellowship, to be invited to take a place at the table. This prompts the question: how could some-body be a Christian without community?

It does not really make sense to think of being a Christian as just an individual matter, 'between me and God'. Rather, it is about being part of a community where the presence of the risen Jesus is tangible, in both the breaking of bread and the way of living. If faith is an encounter with Jesus, then this is where the encounter primarily happens.

And yet ... Some people have little or no link with a commun-ity of Christians yet, each day, in prayer and meditation, they re-late intimately with the Lord. Other people feel unwanted in the church, feel excluded or inadequate perhaps, and yet they be-lieve. Others again, who does not go to church, meet Christ each day in the faces of other people. It does seem that Christian faith can exist without church.

This has to be acknowledged. Maybe we could rephrase it and say that a Christian without community is a Christian in search of community. And often it is the community's own lack of welcome and inclusion that drives faith inward. But the point stands, that faith is not only an inward affair of the heart. While intensely personal, it is not meant to be private.

This challenges the trend towards 'believing without belong-ing' characteristic of spirituality today. It also challenges the tend-ency within church to privatise faith where, for instance, Mass is a private devotion and Christian living is a matter of 'saving my soul'. Christianity without community does not make sense. Faith is meant to be with others and for others.

This brings me to the following key point; church is meant to be an *experience*. Church is an experience of community, togeth-erness, belonging, that becomes an experience of Jesus. In the experience of community with others who are also drawn, a per-son encounters the risen Jesus and is filled with faith and hope. In the experience of belonging, a person is inspired with a sense of mission to make their living a testimony to the good news of the gospel.

It is possible that a person could be taking part in the church without having the experience. Their faith could be a private affair, just for themselves. They could be going through the routines, but without the spirit. In the case of a minister of the church, they could be preoccupied with maintaining structures and services. And it is possible that a person might leave the church not knowing there is an experience to be had.

*Structure*

So, church is a community, centred on the Eucharist, oriented to mission. It is not primarily a building, a structure, an institution, a multinational organisation, a hierarchy. Yet these are what people see. Many people, both outside and inside the church, think that they are what church is. But they are all secondary.

At the same time there is a structure and there is a hierarchy. One way of putting it would be to say that the church is a community structured for mission. The structure, in the sense of the leadership or hierarchy, is meant to be at the service of community and mission. It is in a facilitating role. Part of this service is ensuring that the church grows ever more faithful to its founding vision, its identity.

In our day we have learned to be critical of institutions, indeed highly suspicious. This applies to the church no less than to other organisations. The leadership structure can be absorbed in another agenda. It can be holding on to 'the dead faith of the living' rather than taking forward 'the living faith of the dead' (phrases coined by the historian of Christianity Jaroslav Pelikan). In a later chapter we will talk about the stance of 'critical loyalty' that this calls for in the believer.

*For reflection*

If church is meant to be an experience, how would you describe what the experience is meant to be? And how does this compare with what has been your own experience?

CHAPTER NINE

# *Eucharist*

While this is a book about Christianity it is being written from a Catholic Church standpoint. In that tradition, Eucharist would seem to be the main thing that Christians do. So a picture of what church is and a picture of what Eucharist is go together. Indeed, the two themes of community and mission are central to both.

At the same time, language is changing. Catholics now speak of Eucharist. Where they used to talk about 'going to Mass' now they talk about 'celebrating the Eucharist'. This indicates that, although it is the same event it always was, it is being seen differently. Or perhaps more significantly, people are seeing themselves differently.

## A caricature

I begin with something of a caricature, though it is not far from the way some people see things. At the centre of Mass is a priest. At ordination he was invested with special spiritual powers. When, at the 'consecration', he pronounces a certain formula of words over the bread and wine on the altar table, they are changed into the body and blood of Christ.

The change is often explained as 'transubstantiation'. It is not an apparent change but a substantial one. It is not a symbolic presence but a real one. Then at 'communion' time, when those present receive of this new reality, they are receiving Christ into their souls. It might be added that, for a long period of history until recently, most people did not partake of communion. Mass very much revolved around the spectacle of the consecration.

Today, increasing numbers of people find this 'change' and 'presence' quite inconceivable. To a neutral onlooker they make little or no sense. The very physical language can be repellent, even suggestive of something cannibalistic. It is still empirically bread and wine, and the empirical is what is real. Even for believers it can be more like a suspension of disbelief – as if, trying hard enough, they will make themselves believe it.

*An Experience*

Christianity is about embodiment, about mystery and about visibility. It is about God present in Jesus of Nazareth. It is about the risen Jesus present in the community called church. It is about his presence in the Eucharistic gathering.

Again we are talking about an experience. So if the belief just described is to make sense, we need to connect with the underlying experience. The following passage that begins the first letter of John in the New Testament offers a key:

> … what was from the beginning, what we have heard, what we have seen with our eyes, what we have looked at and touched with our hands, concerning the word of life – this life was revealed and we have seen it.

The author is writing about Jesus, more than half a century after his death and resurrection. There is a strong sense of an experience that is as real 'now' as it was 'then'. It is more than an historical memory that did not fade. It is about a presence. It is about Jesus risen, and present as risen, present from the further sphere of existence into which he has entered. Whether it is 50, 500 or 2,000 years later makes no difference. When Christians today gather, to do as Jesus instructed them, it is the same encounter, the same experience, the same presence. There is a oneness in time.

In the last chapter, I said that community is where this encounter happens. Eucharist is the place where the Christian community gathers. It is the place where the experience is especially available. 'Where two or three are gathered in my name, I am there among them' (Matthew 18:20).

*A together experience*

These words from Matthew point us to a quality of the experience that Eucharist is meant to be. It is that it is a 'together experience'. Jesus said: 'Do this in memory of me. And so, we do as he asked; not individually but together. The Eucharist is a joint, shared, collective action. When there is a strong sense of doing it together, it becomes an experience. It becomes an experience in which we encounter Jesus, risen and present.

Two issues arise here, one about passivity, the other about

privacy. First, passivity. People have been conditioned into thinking that Eucharist is something to be watched – something that the priest does, that happens on the altar. This comes from the days of the Latin Mass: people participated as best they could (saying the rosary, reading the missal), but they were spectators, looking on. Expressions such as 'receiving' communion are suggestive of this passivity.

Second, privacy. Eucharist in this mode becomes a private devotion, transacted between the individual and the Lord. Without belittling the depth of such devotion, the scene might be compared to that at a cinema. There are many people, in the same space, with the same focal point; but they are separate. This is how it has been – multiple acts of individual prayer in a common space. Again notice the language; people talked of 'going to' Mass, 'getting' Mass, 'hearing' Mass.

It is striking, then, that the word 'I' rarely occurs in the ritual. With a couple of exceptions, the prayers are communal: 'We worship you, we give you thanks.' 'We believe in God …' 'Our Father…' 'Give us this day our daily bread…' 'We thank you for counting us worthy…' 'Grant that we … become one body, one spirit in Christ.'

To say that Eucharist is something 'we do' is the opposite of privacy (because it is 'we') and of passivity (because we 'do'). There is a big mindset issue here. Today, it is this active togetherness that facilitates the experience. If active togetherness is lacking, the experience is less accessible. And it becomes much harder to believe.

*We gather*

So we ask, not so much: 'What happens?' as: 'What is it that we do? And what happens when we do it?' The question is not what the priest does, but what we do, led by the priest. I will explain it in terms of four moments, four actions. In this I am trying to depict the ideal situation and I am conscious that the reality often falls short.

The first thing people do is to gather. It is not about turning up, like at a bus stop. It is about assembling. As the last chapter said, this is what 'church' means in the New Testament. It is the gathering or assembling of people for the Eucharist. So this moment is far from inconsequential. It is the first act of being church, an act of self-expression.

So we would expect a sense of occasion, similar to other festive gatherings in life. We look for elements of greeting, welcoming, socialising. We expect a feeling of belonging, of community, of being at home. If it is not like this, what does that say about how the people present see themselves?

Even though Eucharist has hardly begun, we are already at the heart of it. 'Where two or three are gathered in my name, I am there among them.' In gathering, there is already presence, real presence. Jesus' risen presence is palpable in how people gather. If there is a human feel to it – warmth, welcome, energy, enthusiasm – there is also a divine feel, a sense of God's welcoming embrace. If such human feeling is lacking, how can there be a feeling of God's welcoming, spirit-filled presence?

*We connect*

The second moment or action is where people together are connecting with the good news of the gospel. They listen to the Word, the scripture, the story of Jesus' life, death and resurrection. This is the story of where Christians come from, the good news that inspires them to gather. When Christians remember where they come from, they remember who they are.

Listening is active, not passive. It is with a view to connecting. The Word is meant to meet people where they are at, to intersect with the real circumstances of real lives. The purpose of the priest's sermon is to help people connect the message to what is going on in their lives. But it is more than an individual exercise. It is meant to build up a shared sense of identity, a sense of the Word uniting all present to a common source of meaning and direction in their lives.

Again, there is presence. It is not just 'words, words, words', but something that happens between people and God. Later in the Eucharist there is a prayer: 'Only say the Word and I shall be healed.' It suggests that, when the Word is spoken and heard, something happens. It might be healing, or enlightenment, or comfort, or awakening, depending on where people are at. In the Word, the risen Jesus, Word of God, is present and active.

*We break bread*

The third moment is around the specific action that Jesus told his followers to imitate. They bring bread and wine to the shared table and say, as he did, a prayer of blessing and thanks ('Eucharist' means giving thanks). Even though the priest does most of the talking, the key thing is that he is speaking on behalf of all. All are praying this together.

It begins with bringing bread and wine to the table. But they are not 'raw materials'. They are symbolic of those present. They represent people's hopes and tears, their joy and failures, their loves, their very lives. When bread and wine are brought forward, we see ourselves in them. We ourselves are placed on the altar. The prayer of thanks (the 'Eucharistic' prayer) is then said over the bread and wine – and over ourselves.

This is the threshold of mystery, the mystery contained in Jesus' words: 'This is my body, this is my blood'. 'This' – not just bread and wine, but also those whose selves have been placed on the altar. The mystery embodied in the bread and wine is twofold. It is the mystery of the risen Jesus present among his followers. And it is the mystery of those followers themselves, his body.

These two aspects of the mystery are held together in a very clear way in the third Eucharistic prayer:

> And so Father, we bring you these gifts. We ask you to make them holy by the power of your Spirit, that they may become the body and blood of your Son …
>
> Grant that we, who are nourished by his body and blood, may be filled with the Holy Spirit and become one body, one spirit in Christ.

We tend to think of communion as receiving the body of Christ into our souls. Saint Augustine, in one of his sermons, has it the other way round. He speaks of our 'being digested into his body and being turned into his members, so that we may be what we receive'.[6] His presence is not something apart from what we are.

*We are sent*

The concluding moment is a sending. The word 'Mass' comes from the Latin *missa*, which is also the word for mission. The final moment of the Eucharist is more than finishing up, just as the first moment was more than turning up. People gathered as church, now they are sent.

Writing about this, Pope John Paul II said: 'We cannot keep to ourselves the joy we have experienced.'[7] There is something here that is akin to gossip; it is only worth knowing if it can be passed on. The experience of Eucharist is not for hoarding. It is an impulse outwards. Eucharist is only completely celebrated when it is lived.

In the gospels, Jesus asked his followers: 'Are you able to drink the cup that I drink?' (Mark 10:38). 'Drinking the cup' here has two senses. It has the sense of communion. And it has the sense of life being a gift-sacrifice, like Jesus'. The sending moment of the Eucharist is the movement from the first of these to the second.

And again, the presence. Now it is Jesus present in the genuine quality of Christian living. The two are inseparable; present in the Eucharistic gathering, present in the witness of people's lives. Perhaps the latter is where others will see Jesus most clearly. Perhaps it is in Christian witness that Jesus is most persuasively 'embodied'. There, he is seen in his body, the community of Christians.

I began by saying that the Eucharist would seem to be the main thing that Christians do. The 'would seem' was deliberate. Maybe the sending is the main thing? Maybe what matters most is the living of faith, for that is what gives substance to the belief in his presence. Without that witness talk of a 'real' presence can itself sound unreal.

*For reflection*
The last chapter talked of church in terms of community and mission. How do you see those two themes reflected in the Eucharist?

## CHAPTER TEN

# *Are People Good or Bad?*

When I look in the mirror what do I see? Beyond the figure, the looks, the expression; what do I see when I see me? And not just me, but any of us. What are you looking at when you look at a human person? Is it beauty or beast, mess or success? Are people fundamentally good or bad? Do we know at all?

And what does God see? The Bible has it that 'humans look on the outward appearance, but the Lord looks on the heart' (1 Samuel 16:7). This chapter is about what God sees in people, which is central to what Christianity has to say. Christianity is a 'take' on the human person. It offers what it understands to be the view from God's perspective, how God sees each one of us.

## *A negative strain*
One version of the Christian view runs as follows. Our first ancestors started off in the Garden of Eden. All was bliss and goodness, but not for long. Through an 'original sin' (more of which in the next chapter), what was good turned sour. Humankind thereafter is in a state of corruption, until it is saved by Christ, who 'pays the price' for its iniquity.

There have been huge theological debates around what happens next. One view says that people are then restored to original goodness, but are still inclined to sin. Another says that they will always be corrupt, but that God will not 'hold it against them'. Overall, the person seems to be caught between the opposing forces of sin and grace. The Reformation yielded the phrase *simul justus et peccator*; both justified and sinner, both saved and corrupt.

The Christian, it seems, is never entirely either good or bad. And yet it is fair to ask: which are we really, at our core? Through it all, the impression is that people come into existence defective in some critical spiritual sense. They are alienated from themselves and lack the capacity to set things right of their own power. They are compromised before they begin and cannot go far without going wrong.

So there has been a sadly negative strain running through

Christianity in how it views the human person. I think the phrase 'good news' captures the spirit of the Christian message, yet more often than not it has felt like bad news. There has been an overriding sense of the person as sinner, their mortal soul forever in danger.

There is a complex history to this, a lot of it about Christianity's interaction with the cultures in which it grew up. And it has coloured our picture of Jesus. It has cast him more as one who died for our sins than as one who lived for our beauty. It has depicted him as one who came to sort out the mess of our past, rather than as one who imagined our future.

I wonder if this is also connected with the authoritarian style of the Catholic church. I am thinking of its moral teachings, how its way has been to tell people what to do and what to think, rather than to encourage conscience and freedom and responsibility. Is this because of an underlying feeling that people cannot be trusted to their own devices? Is it because of a suspicion that the dark forces within are too powerful; that we are more bad than good?

*Something more*

There is, undoubtedly, an amount of realism about this view, in that it does not gloss over the dark side. There is another, non-theological version of who we are that has interesting parallels. It holds that our original state is not one of harmony but of self-interest. We are basically beings who look out for ourselves. This leaves us headed for collision. One person's desire is going to come up against the desire of another; there are going to be conflicts of interest.

In this view, that is why we have what we call society, to manage the conflicts. We need laws, social controls that we all contract into. We need this for our own sake, so that we can pursue our interests to the maximum degree possible without destroying one another. It is all quite pragmatic. Altruism or other-centredness does not come into it. There is no obligation to others beyond what the law demands; anything further is optional.

This makes for a particular way of reading the golden rule, 'Do to others as you would have others do to you.' In this reading, you treat others well for the sake of your own welfare. It is about the original self-interest learning to become enlightened self-interest. But all the while, what we are at our core is self-interested beings.

A lot of people would want something more than these versions of themselves. Many would want to say that each of us is more than a sinner and more than a self-interested being. To elaborate, let me pose a question. Which of the two, morality or religion, seems to you to go deeper in the human person? I know the question may lack definition, but when it is posed simply as it is, the great majority of people say 'morality'. Why?

For instance, many older parents worry because their teenagers do not go to Mass. Let us ask them; would you prefer your son/daughter to go to Mass but turn out a bad person, or not go to Mass yet turn out a good person? The answer is clear. In other words, we have a deep aspiration about ourselves as 'good persons'. 'Good' here doesn't mean 'goodie goodie'. It is more than being law-abiding. It is not just being 'nice'. It is a deep spiritual aspiration.

This suggests to me that, when we look in the mirror, the 'me' we see may not yet be there. We see what we may become. We see something more than self-interest or material flourishing, important as these are. We see possibility, the possibility to be the best person we can be. We can see that there is a 'pearl of great price' to be found.

*What does God see?*
So, back to the question, 'What does God see when God sees me?' The answer begins quite simply. What God sees is something of God's own making. A good analogy would be that of a mother or father looking on their newborn child, and thinking perhaps: 'You, whom I behold, are of me.'

God looks on us as creator to created. What God sees is one whose being originates in God's own self. This is not meant to confuse the fact of our originating in our parents' sexual union (as if God made it a threesome in the bed). It is saying that our origins are more than physical.

Sometimes a child will ask: 'Where was I before I was in Mummy's tummy?' Some parents reply, 'You were in God's pocket!' It is an appealing image. Each of us originates as an idea

on God's part, an intention of God. We come into being with a
resounding 'Yes!' from God's heart. This is reflected in the Book
of Genesis' poetic depiction of God making the world. The refrain
at each moment is: 'God saw that it was good.' God delights in
what God creates.

Are we good or bad? This answer is clear. We are good, but
in a very specific sense of 'good'. It is not moral goodness, for
that comes later with self-discipline. It is not physical goodness,
for we may well be born with imperfections. We are good because God delights in us. Because God loves us, we are loveable.
Because God delights in us, we are delightful.

When we say: 'I am good' we are saying that we are God's
creation, an expression of God's heart and imagination. We are
saying that we are God's delight. In some such vein Thomas
Merton spoke of what he called le *point vierge*, the virgin point of
our being:

> At the centre of our being is a point of nothingness which
> is untouched by sin and by illusion, a point of pure truth,
> a point or spark which belongs entirely to God … This lit-
> tle point of nothingness and of absolute poverty is the
> pure glory of God in us … It is like a pure diamond, blaz-
> ing with the invisible light of heaven.[8]

### A mixed bag

That last point is basic. In the eyes of Christianity, there is nothing as deep and fundamental, nothing as original or as intrinsic
to our being. But nevertheless, 'What God sees when God sees
me' also includes the unfolding story of what happens in our
lives. God sees both what God made and what we make of what
God made us. That includes darkness as well as light.

When we look at a newborn baby, we see grace and goodness. But later on, when life unfolds and takes its toll, through
different circumstances and experiences, through moral courage
and moral capitulation, we come to be a very mixed bag indeed.
In the words of Shakespeare:

> The web of our life is of a mingled yarn, good and ill to-
> gether; our virtues would be proud if our faults whipped
> them not; and our crimes would despair if they were not
> cherished by our virtues.[9]

There are people who hate themselves. Through life's experiences they can see no good. They cannot access the cherishing power of their virtue. And there are those who love themselves too much. Their life has blinded them to their own shortcomings. They cannot access their own humility.

What does God see? Or perhaps the question now is: how does God see us in light of the ups and downs? What does God make of the mix? Does God see us as we see ourselves? If we despise ourselves or if we glorify ourselves, can we presume that we are aligned with God's view of ourselves?

*Good news*
Christians find their response in the gospel, in the story of Jesus of Nazareth. But they can get it wrong. They can make it sound like: 'You (human being) have become bad, but now the remedy is here; you have been bought back, paid for with Christ's blood.' That does not represent the thrust of the gospel.

What we have in Jesus is the human expression of how God sees us. So, how does Jesus see people? I would say that the big thing happening in the gospels is about how people come to see themselves when they see how Jesus sees them. In an earlier chapter I spoke about this encounter in terms of Jesus' compassion for people.

The best illustration, to my mind, is Jesus' characteristic action of sharing table with so-called 'outcasts and sinners' (itself the origins of Eucharist). The 'logic' of what he was at is both simple and profound. The 'outcasts' were just that – rejected, ostracised by society because of what they did or who they were. As so often happens, rejection is internalised, so that people no longer believe in themselves, no longer have hopes for themselves.

Jesus' sharing table is his act of seeing them differently. It is like the story of the prodigal returning, the son saying 'I am sinner' and the Father saying 'You are son' (Luke 15). People brought to their encounter with Jesus this overwhelming sense of their own inadequacy. And what they encountered was a different perception of themselves. It was as if they looked in a mirror and were surprised by beauty.

Or again, think of the story of the woman who committed adultery (John 8). The scribes and Pharisees would punish her with stoning, according to the law. They define her by her past.

'You are sin' is their final statement about her. But Jesus' reaction says to her: 'You are future.' He defines her as possibility, as hope. This was the pattern with so many who encountered him. How they saw themselves was transformed by how he saw them.

We are each invited into a similar encounter, to learn to see what God sees. We are called to see ourselves as God's cherished creation. We are called to see ourselves, notwithstanding our fallings from grace, as possibility and as future. The inmost core of Christian faith is not our believing in God but God believing in us. Believing in God and believing in ourselves go together.

*For reflection*
If the above expresses the Christian view of the human person, then do you think that in general people are too hard or too easy on themselves?

CHAPTER ELEVEN

## *How Original is Original Sin?*

The topic of original sin was in the background of the last chapter's discussion of whether people are good or bad. What I want
to present here is a way of thinking about this Christian doctrine
that might make sense to people today.

*Past or present?*
We associate original sin with Adam and Eve in Genesis, the
first book of the Old Testament. It is worth noting, though, that
the term original sin only appears well after the New Testament
was written. What we have in Genesis is a way of looking at the
world that only much later was given this designation.

We know today that the story of Adam and Eve is not an historical report. It is not as if somebody was on the spot and the
story was then handed on and written down. In fact, the story is
not mainly about past events at all. It is an effort to understand
what is going on in the present.

In the Book of Jeremiah, written around 600 BC, the prophet
asks:

> Run to and fro through the streets of Jerusalem,
> look around and take note!
> Search its squares and see if you can find one person
> who acts justly and seeks truth –
> so that I may pardon Jerusalem (5:1).

One person! People in the present are shaken by the lack of
goodness and integrity, by how pervasive wickedness is. They
ask: was it always thus? Their sense is that there never was a
time when it was otherwise. This is universal. It is the human
condition. It goes back to our origins.

And so the story of Adam and Eve. It is not an historical
record, but a story that seeks to capture this sense. The focus is
not on explaining what happened then. It is on trying to understand what is happening now. The story is an effort to set what
is happening now into a worldview where it makes some kind
of sense.

We could carry out the same kind of exercise ourselves. We can look around us and see the injustice in the world; how much of life is governed by self-interest; the numbness to human need. We can observe the failure of integrity, of fidelity, of moral courage. And we can ask: was it ever otherwise? And if it was always thus, what does that tell us about ourselves, as human beings, as a human race?

Of course there is goodness in the world. But there is so much of the opposite that it does look as if there is some inbuilt 'fault' in us. Thus John Henry Newman wrote:

> The human race ... is out of joint with the purposes of its Creator. This is a fact, a fact as true as the fact of its existence; and thus the doctrine of what is theologically called original sin becomes to me almost as certain as that the world exists.[10]

That is the first idea about original sin. Reflecting on our human story, we are led to the conclusion that moral failure is so endemic as to go back to our origins as a species.

*Freedom*

The second idea, which we also find in Genesis, is that it does not quite go back to our origin. I recall the point from the last chapter: what is original is the goodness of what God created. So, whatever else original sin means, it is not that it is the most fundamental thing about us.

This again echoes with our experience. With all the evil that seems so endemic, we also sense a core of goodness in ourselves. People may differ in how they gauge the balance of good and evil in us. But the biblical view is that the goodness runs deeper and is more original. God did not create us with something wrong with us.

This leads into the third idea, which is freedom. Freedom is what distinguishes the emergence of humanity. At every other point of evolution, what emerged (plant, animal and so on) would follow its inbuilt, pre-programmed instructions. But humanity was different. Here were beings who could think about things, think about themselves and decide about themselves. Here were beings who could make choices, choices that would shape the world and shape themselves.

It is not as if the first thing that the first human being did was wrong. It is more about something 'fallible' in what we are. If there is freedom, then there are the twin possibilities of becoming or failing to become. The sense of 'original sin' is that the realisation of the negative potential of freedom (which we sense within us and see all around us) is something that goes back to our origins.

### The universal situation

But how is it that whatever happened back then is a universal human condition? First, look at that word 'Adam'. In the Hebrew it is not an individual person's name, but almost always a collective term for humankind. For instance, this is its meaning in Genesis 2:7: 'The Lord God formed man ('adam') from the dust of the ground.' It is 'man' in the sense of humanity. It derives from the word for earth. 'Adam' means 'the earth creature'.

It is a neat way of saying that we are all there in the garden. The story is not so much about an original event. Rather, the story of an original event is a symbolic way of expressing something universal about our human condition. We are all there. We are all 'formed by God', invited into being and becoming. And we are all part of the failure in human becoming.

When it comes to how this came to be, we find that different ways of explaining it are possible. Some of the explanations we have inherited are less than satisfactory. On the other hand, some recent exploration of the question is quite stimulating.

A traditional view of original sin is that we are 'born wrong'. We have contracted a moral and spiritual defect in the very moment of procreation. It is not yet something that is our own fault. But it is a moral disorder that predisposes us to sin and leaves us in need of divine rescue if we are not to be 'lost'.

Saint Augustine (c400 AD) is much associated with this, and it is very much linked with his negativity around sexuality. The sin of the first human beings is transmitted through the generations physically in sexual intercourse. He comments that it is no accident how a new-born baby cries long before it laughs. The crying baby, he says, is 'a prophet of its own future misfortunes'.[11] In this mindset, baptism comes to be seen as the remedy; only then is the new human being graced.

A different approach, developed in contemporary theology, thinks in terms of human freedom and of the 'situation' in which it finds itself in the world. Freedom, it says, is not absolute. We cannot just do whatever we want. Our freedom is to some extent pre-determined by the situation and circumstances we find ourselves in.

Our situation includes our physical or mental or emotional capacities. It includes our socio-economic position. It includes our past experiences. These factors are given, they are there before we act. Freedom is about our 'response-ability'. It is what we make of a situation and circumstances that are not of our choosing.

The idea of original sin is about the 'situation' we are born into, the world we come into. That world includes the sin and guilt of all who have gone before us. Along with all the goodness, the accumulated wrongs of centuries and millennia have made the world we enter into what it is. 'God's Grandeur' by Gerard Manley Hopkins reflects this:

> Generations have trod, have trod, have trod;
> And all is seared with trade; bleared, smeared with toil;
> And wears man's smudge and shares man's smell.

It has been called 'the sin of the world'. There is a sense of everything being contaminated by the accumulation; nothing escapes it. But the accumulation of evil is not just out there in the world, apart from us. The point is that it enters into our freedom, before we act.

A useful image might be that of passive smoking. I enter a room where people have been smoking. I myself am not smoking, but the nicotine (literally) enters into me, and it compromises my health. I did not do anything other than just be there; yet I am compromised. Likewise the sin of the world enters into the fabric of my being.

It is as if we carry the ambiguous history of human freedom in our genes. We carry something of its grandeur and goodness, but we are also compromised by its dark side and perversions. Not only is freedom fallible because of its twin possibilities. But also, there is something of an inclination to evil with which we have been corrupted by the history of humanity.

We find that we are divided within ourselves. In the eloquent reflection of Saint Paul: 'I do not understand my own
actions. For I do not do the good I want, but the evil I do not
want is what I do' (Romans 7:15, 19). The sad fact is: each of us is
going to add to the woe in the world.

*Plan A*
Original sin is a Christian idea, yet most of what I have said so
far is persuasive on its own merits. Original sin, in the sense presented here, is an interpretation of the human condition that makes
a lot of sense. But we have not really talked about Christianity
yet. We have yet to get to the heart of the Christian idea of original sin.

For Christians, there is another and even bigger dimension
to the idea. Original sin is not just an interpretation of the
human condition. Rather, it is part of a larger reflection on the
event of Jesus Christ in the world. Original sin is not a free-
standing theory, but part of a bigger worldview.

Again here, our received ideas are not always helpful. We
have the impression that Christ is God's 'Plan B'. 'Plan A' was
creation, the garden of Eden. But we messed up: the 'original'
sin. So God had to act again, to rescue us from the mess we had
got ourselves into. Baptism, then, is our entry ticket into Plan B.

Logically, this means that, were there no mess of original sin,
there would be no Christ either – because no longer needed. In
this way of thinking, the Incarnation is an afterthought, addi-
tional to the initial script. And if no Christ, then no Trinity
either. This does rather take the ground from under Christianity.

Let us look at it another way, starting with Jesus. The experience of people in the gospels is that, when they encounter Jesus,
they come to see the true face of God. We explored this already,
his compassion and his liberating effect in people's lives. We
saw how, meeting him, people experienced a God bent upon
humanity. People were put in touch with God's passion that all
God's people would know all the goodness of being a human
being.

In Jesus the full dimensions of God's creative process unfold.
In this sense, it is the gospels that tell the story of creation, not
Genesis. In the gospels we have the full revelation of what

creation is all about. Saint Paul writes of God's plan for creation, to unite all things in Christ (Ephesians 1:10). From this angle, the harmony of the garden of Eden is not so much our original state as it is our ultimate destiny.

Now look at original sin in this light. The sin of the world means that all of this is experienced differently than if history had been otherwise, than if freedom had not failed itself. Because of the sin of the world, God's 'Christ-directed' project of creation is experienced as forgiveness, as reconciliation, as justification, as salvation. Because of sin we encounter Christ, not simply as God's self-giving, but as God's forgiving self-giving.

But the plan was always Christ. The Incarnation is not a second thought, a reaction to unforeseen circumstances. It is first in God's intentions. God's creative process was always oriented to this self-giving to humanity, this unity with humanity. In a sense, the Incarnation is eternal and not just historical. Thus the start of John's gospel: 'In the beginning was the Word ... All things came into being through him.' Christ is the heart of creation from the start. We see this revealed when 'the Word became flesh' (John 1:14).

Another defect of Plan B thinking is that it gives the impression of discrete divine interventions. It portrays a God who has to intervene, to meddle with God's own creative process. It is as if God did not realise what might happen, as if God's original initiative was flawed, not properly thought through.

Plan B thinking also makes for exclusivity. It hinges on a temporal sequence; first creation, then sin, then salvation. That leads in turn to thinking that only some people are saved, namely those of sinful humanity who avail of salvation through baptism. This excludes all who lived before Jesus and all who never knew of him – which is most of humanity.

*Original grace*
It is grace that is original, not sin; the grace of existence, the grace of creation. This grace carries a sense of promise, a blessed prospect of becoming whole. The promise comes to fruition in Jesus, where its full dimensions unfold. A reflection on time and timelessness will help to develop this thought further.

The creation of the universe and its evolution is also the cre-

ation of time, of history. But the Creator is the God of timelessness, eternally present, eternally 'now'. At the intersection of
time and timelessness, this God holds in a single gaze all of
what unfolds historically. For us, existence is step by step, past-
present-future. For God it is all at once.

In this perspective, God's original act and its subsequent unfolding are one. It is not so much that God created the world
(and then came back to fix it) as that God is creating the world.
What for God is an eternal single action is for us an unfolding
process. And at the nucleus of this eternal-now action is Christ.
Christ is not a subsequent revision of a previous action, but the
original intention. From eternity, creation, Incarnation and final
fulfilment are one.

This puts original sin in its place, as it were, by bringing us to
a full picture of the 'situation' of our freedom. It is not just that
our situation is pre-determined by the sin of the world and our
freedom compromised. Also, and more fundamentally, our situation is determined by grace. This is what is most original.

It is not accurate to say that we are born with original sin. To
talk of original sin in that way is to talk of an abstraction, to abstract from the actual world we inhabit. What we are born into is
grace – into a world created by God to be graced in Christ, and
destined to be ultimately transformed into the fullness of God's
intention. Originally, we are 'graced' to be part of this.

But also we are compromised in our freedom by the sin of
the world. The two forces, though, are not equal. As we see
God's creative process unfold in Christ, we see that ours is a forgiven existence, a healed humanity. That is how we are born.
Even if we cry before we laugh, others rejoice at our birth, as
they behold our beauty. Baptism is our celebration of this.

But this is the situation for all people, not just for Christians.
Even if God's creative purpose only becomes clear in time, it is
true for all at all times. For all are held in God's single gaze.
Regardless of whether they knew or know of Christ, all are in
the same situation before God.

*For reflection*
How does this presentation of original sin compare with your
own thinking? What questions does it raise for you?

CHAPTER TWELVE

# Why Did Jesus Die?

When talking about original sin, I said that the Christ event was not a rescue plan on the part of God. And in a number of chapters I have been saying that God's grace is universal, bigger than the Christ event. Ideas such as these query some of our traditional thinking and language about what took place in the life, death and resurrection of Jesus.

In this chapter I want to reflect on some of the language and images we have inherited. In particular, I will reflect on how we talk about what was achieved through Jesus' death on the cross.

## Inherited images

I will begin by listing some of the terms and images involved. We talk about 'sacrifice'. We say that God gave up his Son on the cross; thereby Jesus is the sacrifice that takes our sins away. We talk about 'redemption'. Jesus was the price paid by God to buy us back from the power of sin, a kind of ransom.

We talk about 'salvation'. By Jesus' death on the cross we are saved from our sins and from the power of sin. We talk about 'atonement'. Jesus is the acceptable sacrifice to God that atones for our sins. We talk about 'satisfaction'. Jesus' death is the offering that is satisfactory to God, that makes satisfaction to God for our sin.

This language is ambiguous, admitting of different meanings. Its best meaning is what I hope to arrive at, but it will be necessary first to clear the way. In other words, this language carries with it meanings and implications that do not do justice to what was happening in Christ.

For example, there is one version of the Christian story which represents it as a battle between God and Satan for the soul of humanity. Because of original sin we are under the power of the devil. Something huge is needed in order to release us. And Jesus is the ransom that God offers to the devil to 're-deem' or buy us back.

Another version says that, in our corrupt state, nothing we can offer to God would be satisfactory reparation for our sin.

But Jesus, being himself divine, is adequate, a satisfactory and acceptable atonement offering. Another version again sees Jesus as representing all of humanity. He stands in our place and 'takes the hit' for us. He is a substitute for us, his is a vicarious sacrifice.

Some of these ideas sound extreme. But there is something in all this language and imagery that has entered into our mentality. It needs to be questioned if we are not to be handicapped with a crude and inadequate understanding of what we believe. To begin with, a number of problems with the language can be set out.

*Difficulties*

First, this language often suggests a picture of our human condition that does not square with our experience. It emphasises in a very strong way our being in a state of sin, captive to sin, spiritually lost and corrupt and condemned. It does not seem at all to affirm the grace of our human condition which we experience daily, whether our allegiance is Christian or otherwise.

The language and imagery seem to be part of the 'Plan B' thinking I spoke of in the last chapter. They seem to imply that the Christ event is a divine afterthought in the face of human sinfulness, rather than God's original intention. So it is said that Jesus was 'sent to save' us. Jesus' purpose is seen as a rescue mission.

A couple of other problems are linked with this. For one, it is connected with thinking of God in ways that are far from satisfactory – a point I will develop in the next chapter. It is also connected with a tendency to see grace in an exclusivist way. If humanity is captive to the power of sin, and if the one sent is the only remedy, then that one is the only access to salvation. Thus Christianity has at times spoken of there being no salvation outside of the church and baptism.

Second, the really big difficulty with this language and imagery is the way in which Jesus is presented. He does not come across as an agent in his own right. He is more like an instrument in implementing God's plans. He is spoken of as the price, the ransom, the sacrifice, the substitute, whereby divine-human relations are restored.

The only way of dealing with the situation of original sin is for God to make amends and bail us out. Jesus is very passive, almost a divine puppet. He is a means to an end, the currency of the transaction. Even if 'passive' is too strong a word, his is certainly far less than a full-blown humanity, such as was portrayed in chapter three above.

Another part of this difficulty is that the Resurrection is marginalised. It is the death of Jesus that achieves God's purposes. His death is the sacrifice, the ransom, the price paid, the satisfaction. In the use of this language and imagery, Jesus' being raised from the dead can appear almost inconsequential. This is how we often unwittingly interpret the words of John's gospel: 'God so loved the world that he gave his only Son' (3:16).

*Another approach*

This is not about abandoning the traditional language, but about coming at it from another angle, in order to arrive at its best meaning. So, to remind ourselves of the underlying question: just what was it that was going on when Jesus died? How do we conceptualise and imagine and articulate what was going on and what was achieved? How do we interpret 'sacrifice' and 'redemption' and 'salvation' in a way that gets over the difficulties just outlined?

We do so by getting back to the starting point. Redemption, atonement and so on: this is 'afterwards' language. It is language that comes after an experience, as an attempt to understand the meaning of what was experienced. It is interpretive language. And it is also metaphorical language, imagery rather than precise definition.

Yet the language, as it is commonly presented, comes across literally and crudely, as if to tell us exactly what happened. It can give the impression that what actually happened was an 'out of the skies' divine intervention. But if we realise that it is metaphorical language, articulated out of an experience, then what we need to do is to go back to what was experienced and trace its development – to follow the trail as it were.

If we do that, then we begin with an ordinary, adult, autonomous human being, Jesus from Nazareth. That is what people encountered and experienced. For the purposes of this chapter, what is notable about him is his self-transcending, self-sacrificing interest in others, especially the most unfortunate and forsaken. People experienced him as a liberating presence in their lives.

Against this background we can go back to our question: what is going on when Jesus dies? Let us go to the night before he dies. After the final supper with his companions, he retires to the garden of Gethsemane. There we have his words addressed to God: 'Not what I want but what you want' (Mark 14:36). These words could have either of two meanings.

It could be that Jesus is struggling to assent to a pre-ordained plan of God's that he would die. Or it could be that he is struggling to assent to the direction he finds that his own life has taken. In the former Jesus is like a pawn in a larger transaction. In the latter he is an adult person coming to terms with the difficult circumstances of his life.

And the latter is the context for talking about the 'sacrifice' of the cross. We are not talking about a pre-planned ransom or atonement. We are witnessing a free decision, a path which Jesus chose. It could have been otherwise. But in the circumstances he found himself in, going to his death appeared to him as the path most faithful to the meaning of his life up to this.

It was a sacrifice in the sense that all of his living had been sacrificial, self-giving, other-centred – his body broken and blood poured out in life-giving commitment to others. It was not God's sacrifice of Jesus, God's sacrificing him to achieve an ulterior purpose of redemption or atonement. It was Jesus' sacrificing of himself, his giving of himself in continuity with all his life's giving.

Again, when Jesus speaks of giving his life as 'a ransom for many' (Mark 10:45), he is not talking about himself as a pawn, as the price to be paid for God's favour to be restored. He is talking about the self-giving that is the heart of who he is – and which people were coming to see as the heart of who God is.

We can still call this 'the will of God'. But it is not God's will in the sense of Jesus submitting as an instrument in a predetermined divine plan. Rather, it is God's will in a real human sense. When a human being courageously accepts the truth of their situation and creatively responds to its possibilities, that itself is the will of God. It is what God wants for each and every human being. It is what God wanted for Jesus.

*The main focus*

We are 'following the trail', beginning with people's experience of Jesus' very human and very extraordinary life, leading into his very human and very extraordinary death. But the next point on the trail is not to speak about this death as redemption or atonement or satisfaction. The next step is resurrection.

It is not that Jesus died and that people immediately saw his death as redemption or atonement. It is that Jesus died and that people then experienced his risen presence among them. That experience in turn gave rise to interpretation. The disciples sought to understand its meaning and significance. It is only from the vantage-point of resurrection that the disciples come to interpret the meaning of Jesus' death.

First up in interpreting the resurrection experience is the conviction that 'God is in this'. Take the very early Christian hymn quoted by Paul in Philippians, chapter two. Jesus 'humbled himself and became obedient to the point of death': his courage and commitment, as set out above. The text continues:

> Therefore God also highly exalted him and gave him the name that is above every name, so that at the name of Jesus every knee should bend ... and every tongue should confess that Jesus Christ is Lord.

Very soon after the resurrection, this is where the trail takes us, before any talk of atonement and the like. And this text itself echoes Isaiah 45:23, where God says: 'To me every knee shall bow, every tongue shall swear.' What in Isaiah is said of God, in Philippians is said of Jesus. The early Christian interpretation of their experience is that Jesus is 'of God', so as to assume this status and to be called 'Lord'.

God is in Jesus. God has spoken, expressed, revealed God's self in Jesus' humble self-giving. In Jesus God has revealed God's self as intimate, faithful, self-giving love for humanity. In Jesus' self-giving we see, not ransom or atonement, but God's self-giving. This is the primary meaning of the cross and resurrection.

Only subsequent to this primary focus does the New Testament speak of Jesus' death as a saving event, with the metaphors of redemption, atonement and so on. That happens when the event of God's love in Jesus is interfaced with the actual circumstances of humanity. Because humanity's actual experience of itself is as a frail, fragile, sinful humanity, the divine self-bestowal in love is experienced also as a reconciling, justifying, saving event.

As the last chapter said, what is primarily an event of love is also experienced as an event of forgiveness. It is here that the language of salvation and redemption enters in, together with all the imagery. But we can see now that the meaning conveyed in these images is not that God was conducting a quasi-commercial transaction through the death of Jesus.

To further illustrate this point, reflect on some moments from the gospels. In Luke 19, what Zacchaeus experiences primarily is the welcoming, generous, unconditional love of Jesus. But, because of the background of how he had been conducting himself, he receives it also as a forgiving, liberating experience. Likewise Peter; his encounter with the risen Jesus is presented as a mutual avowal of love (John 21). But it is also, because of the betrayal that went before, a moment of reconciliation and reunion.

First there is the experience of God's love in Jesus. Second there is the further interpretation of this, in the light of humanity's sinful story, as a forgiving love. When we put all the emphasis on sin, God's love is relegated backstage somewhere. We end up with seeing Jesus' death as the cold transaction of a God of ransom and atonement, instead of the perfect human manifestation of a God of love.

*For reflection*
In the light of this chapter, what do you think it means to say that Jesus died for our sins?

CHAPTER THIRTEEN

# Images of God

The question 'Who is God?' runs through the chapters of this book and is perhaps the biggest question of all. Already we have talked about the true face of God being revealed in the life of Jesus and of how God is then understood as Father, Son and Spirit. We have talked about God's intentions for humanity and for creation, as revealed in the Christ event.

Here I want to focus further on the question, for there is more to be said. I want to say something more about the kind of knowledge of God that Christianity offers, and to situate this in relation to the knowledge that others enjoy. Sometimes Christians themselves misrepresent the kind of understanding of God that Christianity brings to the table.

And I want to talk about who God isn't – the misrepresentations of 'God' that we are burdened with. For instance, the 'old man in the sky': where did that come image come from? Was it, perhaps, from Michelangelo's painting in the Sistine Chapel of God and Adam? And where did he get it from? We move closer to who God is when we challenge ourselves to move beyond our more inadequate images.

## Universal access
Back in 1870, the First Vatican Council declared that God can be known with certainty, through the things that are created, with the natural light of human reason. The declaration has been the subject of much debate, but there is just one point that I wish to focus on. It is the implication that every human being is competent and qualified when it comes to talking about God.

God is within the range of ordinary human experience ('the things that are created') and God can be accessed when we reflect on that experience ('reason'). Thus, everybody is to be respected as an equal partner in the conversation about God. Each person is an authority on the subject. This echoes with our discussion in earlier chapters of 'spirituality', of 'grace' and of 'faith' as universal phenomena, bigger than any religion.

There is, of course, a huge range in what people say about God. The variety of religions in the world and the manifold

forms of spirituality testify to this. Some of it represents an enriching diversity of perspective, some of it an arena of disagreement, conflict and contradiction. It is not surprising that it
should be so.

Compare a group of people having a chat about an absent ac-
quaintance. It may be gossip, but often it is just trying to figure
out that person. Such conversation highlights how each of us is
more opaque than transparent. If it is so hard to figure out another person, all the more so the one we call God. Thus the Book
of Wisdom concludes: 'It is hard enough for us to work out what
is on earth, laborious to know what lies within our reach; who,
then, can discover what is in the heavens?' (9:16).

So we talk about the mystery of God. On the one hand, God
is within the range of human experience; God is self-manifest-
ing. And yet, on the other hand, God is beyond our thoughts,
more than our imagining, greater than our grasp. God is universally accessible, but also ineffable, unspeakable.

One medieval definition of God was 'that than which a
greater cannot be thought'. We might add that God cannot even
be thought, let alone expressed. At the end of any discussion of
God there is a sense of the inadequacy of words. Our human
language and human metaphors are all we have; they help and
they fall short. To quote Augustine: 'We are talking about God;
so why be surprised if you cannot grasp it. I mean, if you can
grasp it, it isn't God.'[12]

If language falls short, silence may draw nearer. Think of the
'great silence' that is at the heart of contemplative monastic life.
Mystical literature talks of the 'cloud of unknowing'. In the
sense of awe and of our own smallness; in the silence and the
unknowing: there is God.

### Self-portrait

This helps us to situate what Christianity has to say. It stands
alongside what others have to say. It does not (or should not)
talk about God as if it had the inside track, as if what it says
trumps everybody else's input. Like everybody else, Christianity speaks from its experience.

Christian talk about God is not abstract but concrete. It is
about an experience. For Christians, 'God' has taken shape in a
way that we can recognise and relate to and talk about coherently.

They do not talk just about 'God'. They talk about the God of Jesus Christ. At least that is what is meant to happen. The reality can fall short – the 'old man in the sky', the mathematical conundrum of a 3-in-1 God, and so on – so much of it abstract theorising rather than articulating a spiritual experience.

The phrase 'the God of Jesus Christ' has two senses. It is about the God that Jesus of Nazareth believed in and spoke about and was inspired by. But it is also about Jesus himself, how he himself was believed to portray or 'incarnate' this God. He expresses 'God' in human terms. This means that we have a human language for talking about God. Jesus Christ is our language for talking about God. John's gospel calls him 'the Word'.

Earlier I mentioned a book entitled *Jesus: Self-Portrait by God*. It is a powerful image. If we think of self-portraits in art, those of Rembrandt come to mind. Over a period of forty years, he painted or drew in the region of eighty portraits of himself. It is a remarkable and fascinating preoccupation; we can only wonder what was going on for him. The portraits are extraordinary for their depiction of his inner life. At times we seem to be looking into his soul.

This brings to life the image of Jesus as God's self-portrait. In one sense we could say that Jesus is portraying God, a living presentation of what God is like. In another sense we could say that God is portraying God's self in Jesus. And something of God's soul comes across. In Jesus, we are in touch with the soul or heart or essence of who God is.

We have seen something of this self-portrait in earlier chapters. We see a God whose primary interest is not God's own name and glory, but whose passion is human beings and how we are together as human beings. I recall somebody once offering a definition of God along these lines, as a passionate pursuit of rightness in all God's creation and among all God's creatures. Christianity professes that Jesus is this passion.

Jesus is the distinctive Christian experience of God. All Christian talk of God comes from here, in particular talk of God as 'Trinity'. Such talk is not a flight into theorising, although it has at times been reduced to that. Rather, Christian God-talk is always Jesus-talk. It is rooted in the 'self-portrait', the soul of God expressed therein, the origin and final destiny of our evolving universe revealed as the dynamic and eternal actuality of Love.

*What God is not*

A lot can be said about 'Who is God?' by stating what God is not. Here we confront some of the 'baggage' in the Christian tradition that cramps our imagining about God. I will be listing a number of images in which Christians themselves have misrepresented God.

The last chapter talked about the imagery of God sacrificing God's son as ransom for our sins. We have been taught to think of this as expressing how much God loves us. But who in their right mind would sacrifice their own child? It echoes the story of Abraham and Isaac, but that story ends with Abraham not sacrificing his son. It is a story of moving away from such an image of God.

Such an image suggests a God who is cold enough to do such a thing, more rational than feeling, more remote and aloof than emotionally caught up in events. When thinking of 'sacrifice' we should think instead of the adult human being, Jesus of Nazareth, deciding to continue to death in the same spirit of self-giving that characterised his whole life. And we should think of that as 'portraying' a self-giving God of overflowing love.

Allied to this, God is not the impassible one that we have imagined – so perfect, that is, as to be beyond feeling and injury. The God portrayed in Jesus is more adequately imagined in terms of passion and compassion. This is a God who is affected by our situation, a God who feels for us. Compared to this, the image of impassibility suggests a God to shrink back from.

Again, we have imagined God to be a God of judgement and punishment. Wherever God is cast in these terms, in scripture, church or elsewhere, it represents our poorer efforts to imagine God. Even where the gospels have Jesus talking in these terms, it says more about the imagination of the authors than anything else. Even Jesus' own disciples fall short in grasping the God he portrayed.

The self-portrait of God in Jesus has no place for judging and punishing. This God is utterly faithful, does nothing other than love, forever forgiving us into our own future and into our best selves. And any anger there is in God – the 'wrath' of God – is the anger of compassion at the frustrating of God's dream by God's people. It is not about a vindictive God; it is about God mourning.

We also fail to do justice to God with our language of omnipotence, power and control – the all-powerful God we speak of. Rather, as Paul puts it: 'The message about the cross is the power of God' (1 Corinthians 1:18). He says that the cross is the great image of God's 'power'. The defenceless nature of the cross is God's self-portrayal, the powerfulness of defencelessness. Coming at the end of Jesus' life, it corresponds to the vulnerability of the infant at the start of his life – again an image of God.

Then there is the way we sometimes speak of 'the will of God'. For instance, a little child dies tragically, and people talk about the will of God. Or somebody contracts a severe illness and people say that God is testing that person. It evokes the image of a puppeteer, manipulating events with a logic we cannot fathom, but which appears more cruel than kind.

But the will of God as 'portrayed' in Jesus is simply what God wants. And what God wants is what God passionately desires. It is that God's creative intent would be fulfilled, that human existence would be everything that God imagined it to be in imagining it into being. There is no sense in Jesus of a God who thinks it would be good to have some suffering as part of the process. This God mourns at suffering, just as Jesus did.

This links with another image we have of God; the meddlesome God. It is already there in the puppeteer above. It was there in the 'Plan B' God of the chapter on original sin. We think of God as making discrete interventions in the processes of human history. We think of God interfering. In our prayers we ask God to interfere.

The God of Jesus Christ is Spirit, within us and among us. This God does not hop in and out of human time, either for God's own reasons or in response to our pressure. Rather, this is the God of timelessness, to whom all time is present at once, who beholds at once all that unfolds in time. God does not come and go, but is constant, passionate presence. Again, Jesus 'portrays' this God.

Finally I might say that this God is not a prisoner of gender (a topic to be discussed later). We have, however, imprisoned God in gender. It runs through the foregoing images of what God is not – the God who sacrifices God's own son; the unemotional God; the God beyond feeling, whose heart cannot be hurt; the judgemental, violent, vindictive God; the all-powerful God; the puppeteer God. Is there not something very male about the imagery?

The words of Isaiah should have been adequate warning. Isaiah says that God is like a warrior who stirs up his fury; and that God is like a woman crying out in labour (42:13-14). The full variety of male and female is needed to speak less inadequately of God. Maybe this is part of what we mean when we say that Jesus is 'fully human'. In him God has painted a fully-rounded self-portrait in human terms, male and female.

In all of these points it is obvious that we cannot but speak anthropomorphically, that is, in human terms and images. All of the words and images fall short; all point but faintly to the reality. But some are better than others. And there is a way of gauging or discerning which is which.

The ever-present possibilities for misrepresenting God have one thing in common. They all lose the connection to Jesus of Nazareth. They speak of God, but the speech has drifted away from the self-portrait. The talk, then, is groundless from a Christian point of view. To do any justice to 'God', our imaging must always be grounded in the self-portrait that is the life, death and resurrection of Jesus of Nazareth. At its core, Christian God-talk is always Jesus-talk.

### A practical knowing

I want to conclude by returning to the phrase I used at the start of the chapter: 'the kind of knowledge of God that Christianity offers'. I have been saying that it is not abstract knowledge, the result of speculation or theorising. It is knowledge that comes from reflection on an experience, the experience of the life, death and resurrection of Jesus. But it is knowledge in another sense also.

Think of two people who have been together in a lengthy, life-giving relationship. Compare the way they knew each other in their early days to the way they know each other now. It is not an information or book kind of knowing. It is existential, the knowing born of living, of commitment, of struggle.

Now look at this passage, where the prophet Jeremiah is talking about justice and injustice; observe the unusual way he speaks of 'knowing' God:

> Woe to him who builds his house by unrighteousness
> and his upper rooms by injustice.
> Did not your father eat and drink and do
> justice and righteousness?
> Then it was well with him.
> He judged the cause of the poor and the needy: then it was well.
> Is not this to know me? says the Lord (22:13, 15-16).

'Is not this to know me?' This knowing is actional. It says that people know God when they live God's passion. In our case it means that Christians know who God is when they live life as portrayed in Jesus of Nazareth. They know God when they themselves portray God. They know God when their lives participate in Jesus' portrayal of who God is.

To live life in this way is to live a life divine. But it is not an ideal imposed from without, an alien divinity. Rather, it concurs with our best version of ourselves. We know who God is when we are our best selves, in the practice of compassion, in the weaving of solidarity. There is a co-incidence between our best selves and the God portrayed in Jesus.

So, what we know of God is not a theory but a practice. The God Christianity believes in is a 'put-into-practice' God. The converse holds too. When God is misrepresented in ways such as described above, the misrepresentation is not just in our imagining, but also in our doing. A powerful, judgemental, unfeeling God coincides with a powerful, judgemental, unfeeling Christian or a powerful, judgemental, unfeeling church.

The knowing is in the living. It is expressed well in the fourteenth century spiritual classic *The Cloud of Unknowing*: 'To our intellect God is incomprehensible; not to our love … By love God can be caught and held, but by thinking never.'[13]

*For reflection*
In what ways does the 'self-portrait' of God in Jesus challenge you in your own images of who God is?

## CHAPTER FOURTEEN

# *God Creating the World*

'I believe in God … creator of heaven and earth.' So begins the Christian creed. But what does it mean? In another time the meaning seemed obvious. But today, with all we have learned about evolution, and the 'big bang' with which it all supposedly began? That is the focus of this chapter – the idea of a creator God.

Many grew up believing that the account on the first pages of the Bible, of God creating the world in six days, was literally true. It was read as if it were the report of somebody looking on at the scene. Incredibly, with all that science has shown, there are still some who maintain that the Book of Genesis account is factually accurate.

Yet, as long ago as 400 years after Christ, Saint Augustine could see through that. He asked: if the sun was created on the fourth day, how could there have been days before the sun? Where did the light and darkness of the previous days come from? Clearly, when reading Genesis we are not dealing with journalism or history or science.

*Creation is now*

A better place to start would be the prophet Isaiah (chapters 40 to 55). Here we are in the sixth century before Christ, about 550. The people of Israel have been deported: 'By the rivers of Babylon there we sat down and there we wept' (Psalm 137). They have lost their home, their land, their temple. It was almost as if they were back in Egypt. All is chaos, desolation, nothingness.

How unexpected, then, are the words which the prophet has God speaking into the people's situation. 'Do not remember the former things, or consider the things of old. I am about to do a new thing; now it springs forth, do you not perceive it?' (43:18-19). Something new, something astonishing, is happening. From the non-existence of Babylon, the people are re-created and they return home.

It is here, in the 'new thing', that creation language is rooted. In the Bible, the Hebrew word for creating is used exclusively of God. It occurs about 50 times in the Old Testament and nearly half the usages are in these twenty or so pages of Isaiah. For example:

Thus says God, the Lord, who created the heavens and stretched them out, who spread out the earth and what comes from it, who gives breath to the people upon it and spirit to those who walk in it ... From this time forward I make you hear new things, hidden things that you have not known. They are created now, not long ago ...' (42:5; 48:6-7).

They are created now, not long ago'; creation is a *present experience*. Out of chaos comes a new thing. In their present circumstances, the people experience the creativity of God, redeeming them (another big word for Isaiah) and redeeming their future. 'Thus says the Lord who created you ... Do not fear, for I have redeemed you; I have called you by name, you are mine' (43:1).

Note the picture of God in this. It is not God doing it all in one unrepeatable act, but God creating and recreating, again and again. It is not God away off in solitary divine splendour, but God here, within the complexities of our human world. It is not God acting in some perfect situation, but God working with us in the messiness of human living.

## Amazement

The final editing of the familiar Genesis account was some time after this. It is not a piece of history, but a liturgical text. It belongs in the context of worship, a hymn of praise to the creator God. It says that in the beginning there was chaos, and the breath of the Lord swept over. What we see in Isaiah is the experience that gives rise to the praise, the present experience of chaos and creation.

So creation-belief is not about the physical origins of the world. It is about a present experience of the creativity of God, the creative power of God-on-our-side. This, as it were, informs the cosmic hymn of praise placed at the start of the Bible. The hymn proclaims that the creativity of God experienced now is the same creativity that underlies the existence of all that is.

Reducing Genesis to a quasi-literal record misses the point entirely. It could even give the impression of a God who made the world and then forgot about it. Genesis is more testimony than history, more prayer than science. Creation is now, the ever new and surprising creativity of God.

I find that the word amazement captures what is going on. People are experiencing the God they believe in as new, surprising, breath-taking. They are amazed at the God they thought they knew. This re-defines their relationship to God. It is now a relationship of amazement, between a God who amazes and a people who are amazed.

It is not one single event, but a pattern. The pattern broadens out to being amazed at the greater dimensions of God's creative power in all creation. It makes for a creaturely posture of amazement, thankfulness and praise. (It is a measure of our distance from the inspiration of the Genesis story that we can read it with hardly a trace of such sentiments.)

### New creation

All this, though, is still no more than a prelude to the Christian belief about God and creation. It forms the backdrop, it shapes the language, it defines the spirit of that belief; but there is more. Christian creation belief is about Jesus Christ.

Theology has tended to separate creation on the one hand and salvation on the other, as if they were two separate events. This relates to what was said in the chapter on original sin, salvation seen as 'plan B', an afterthought to the original creation. But in the reflection on Isaiah above, creation is a saving experience. It is not a far-off event back then, but a liberation experienced here and now.

In the Christian view, God's creative intent comes to full expression in Jesus. Paul says: 'If anyone is in Christ, there is a new creation' (2 Corinthians 5:17). The pages of the gospels are inhabited with women and men who found themselves re-created in their encounter with Jesus. They were liberated into a new self and a new future. They were amazed.

The core of it, as presented earlier, is resurrection. In Jesus' cry on the cross – 'My God, why have you forsaken me?' – we can hear the echo of Babylon. Into the chaos and desolation of the cross, into the nothingness of the tomb, God breathes life. God creates, does a new thing. And here too, the response is amazement:

> Peter got up and ran to the tomb; stooping and looking in, he saw the linen clothes by themselves; then he went home, amazed at what had happened (Luke 24:12).

In the Acts of the Apostles, a spirit of amazement is palpable as his followers testify to Jesus risen. On reflection, it crystallises into the realisation that, in Jesus risen, we are in touch with the whole purpose of God's creative endeavour.

> With all wisdom and insight (God) has made known to us the mystery of his will, according to his good pleasure that he set forth in Christ, as a plan for the fulness of time, to gather all things up in him (Ephesians 1:8-10).

Creation – this human world, in its vast expanse of time and space – is God's venture. Creation is God's work-in-progress. Its pattern is amazement; future out of desolation, new life out of destruction, hope out of despair. Its pattern is surprising new-ness and transformation. Jesus' resurrection is the prototype. It is the anticipation of the final transformation.

In its final pages, the New Testament counterpoints the first page of Genesis. The author of the Book of Revelation beholds 'a new heaven and a new earth', where God and God's people – divinity and humanity – will be one, where every tear is wiped away, where death is no more. And the voice from the heavenly throne proclaims: 'See, I am making all things new' (21:5).

We can re-read the seven days of Genesis from this view-point, not literally but imaginatively. The first five days repre-sent the vast process of evolution form the 'big bang' to the emergence of life on earth. The sixth day represents the millen-nia of human history. And the seventh day represents rest, in the sense of 'recreation' – God's creative process completed, noth-ing now but praise and joy.

*Science and religion*
I started with the question, what does the Christian creed mean by: 'I believe in God, the creator of heaven and earth?' What fol-lowed above is the sketch of a reply. It depicts God as a creative, liberating, transforming presence in the unfolding story of God's world.

This in turn offers new possibilities for appreciating the interac-tion between Christianity and modern science. To argue that Genesis is literally true obviously makes for conflict and conflicting claims. The approach I have been sketching takes us beyond con-flict. It suggests that theology and science have different interests.

Theology has mainly a human interest. Its focus is the drama of society and history, especially in the present tense. It is interested in the presence of God within this human drama. Science is more interested in the physical world, its origins and development, the patterns and laws of its evolution.

Science and theology share in common an awe and wonder in the face of what they study and what they uncover. ('God' is theology's name for that wonder.) But the questions that they ask are different and, likewise, the methods and their respective languages. Conflict arises when this distinction is confused – when theology purports to answer scientific questions about how the world began, or when science claims to answer theological questions about the meaning and purpose of the universe.

I do not wish to overstate this. Science does open out into the big questions about existence. It does generate a profound sense of mystery that may be the threshold of faith. On the other hand, of course, it can prompt the sense of an impersonal universe, random and cruel. But the differentiation of different questions proper to each allows for dialogue and mutual enrichment.

It may also allow for synthesis. I think for instance of Teilhard de Chardin, the Jesuit scientist of the early twentieth century. He sought to marry Christian belief and evolutionary theory. He spoke of the universe as an evolution. But he saw evolution to be striving in the direction of spirit and of the personal. He saw this process reaching perfection in the convergence of all things in Christ, the 'Omega point' of creation.

*Re-imagining God*
For a long time the insights of modern science have been felt as a threat by religion – from the time of Galileo to that of Darwin, and after. But things have moved on. Now we can think of religion learning from science and being enriched. We can think of science as inviting Christianity into new ways of seeing God.

God did not create the world in one perfect act. It is more accurate to think of God as creating evolution! Ours is not a puppet-theatre world where everything is managed according to a pre-conceived blueprint. Our world is an open process. God creates a world released to discover its own possibilities. It is an arena of improvisation, a world set free to create itself. The 'let there be …' refrain of Genesis is God's saying 'let it be' to the evolutionary process.

If such is the case, then chaos and unpredictability are going to be part of the process. There will be wonder and delight, novelty and surprises. Equally, there will be blind alleys, malfunctions, cruelties and destruction. The alternative of a God-in-control would mean no pain or struggle. But there would also be no drama or transformation or newness.

The image of God letting be does not mean God retires to look on from afar. The image is about presence, not absence. God accompanies the evolutionary process. God's Spirit is the 'within-ness' of evolution. God is with creation in its exertion to become. And God's presence is infinite compassion, unfathomable promise, inviting the world to become itself.

The imagery is that of resurrection, the archetype of all evolution. Out of chaos comes new creation. Death is breaking through to new life. Turbulence becomes transformation. Or there is the parallel image of childbirth in Paul's letter to the Romans. 'We know that the whole creation has been groaning in labour pains until now' (Romans 8:22). Throughout, God is 'ever newness'.

### Re-imaging ourselves

In the drama of creation, the human being is centre stage. The emergence of humanity is the emergence of consciousness. This, it has been said, is the greatest single event since the big bang. Evolution is now a self-conscious process. With this, humankind is an active agent in the evolutionary process. The creature is also a co-creator.

Now the world can participate consciously in its own unfolding. There is a partnership between God and humanity in shaping what the future will bring. It is true that the advent of freedom does multiply the unpredictability and risk in creation. But this can also be seen as an intensification of God's own trust in the process. Human freedom is God's creative risk.

Sometimes 'freedom' and 'God' can appear to be opposites, as if any mention of God dilutes autonomy and turns freedom into dependence. But in this view freedom is itself a grace, it is bestowed by God. It is not apart from God, it is our very relationship to God. Freedom is the expression of God's creativity.

And with the emergence of freedom, a new horizon comes into view. The future opens up as the possibility of a community of love. With human consciousness and freedom, creation has become a capacity for receiving God. There is now the prospect that divine energy – or 'love' – may permeate all the relationships and interactions within the world.

As Christianity sees it, human beings realise this possibility by themselves taking on board the logic of evolution. The logic is that of resurrection, of breakthrough, from death to new life, from chaos to new creation. In this logic, human life is patterned around transformation – transcending self, letting go in order to be created anew. This brings evolutionary process to its newest moment yet.

The New Testament abounds in this mentality. For Paul, baptism is dying into Christ's death, so that 'we too might walk in newness of life'. The 'old self' is crucified and gives way to a 'new self' which is constantly being renewed and transformed (eg Romans 6; Romans 12; Ephesians 4; Colossians 3). Again, the God of novelty and surprise is the constant presence, the Spirit energising the emergence of higher forms of life.

This leads into a theme of responsibility. Human beings are evolution-become-conscious, co-creators, God's partners in the unfolding story of the universe. We are all partners in transformation, blessed with a share of divine creativity. We are all called to make the world more like the place that it is divinely imagined to be.

In conclusion, this may give us a way to think about miracles. Usually a miracle means a supernatural intervention, outside the laws of nature. But we are talking here of God being creatively present in the world, in its resurrection pattern of transformation and newness. Maybe we should be thinking about the miracle that is existence itself, with its daily capacity to amaze us?

*For reflection*
What have you experienced or reflected upon in your own life that would lead you to believe in the creative power of God?

CHAPTER FIFTEEN

# *Suffering and God*

'Why suffering?' may well be the biggest question of all. So much agonising has gone into it over millennia – the Book of Job in ancient times; more recently the popular book, *When bad things happen to good people.* Maybe the clearest thing about suffering is that no clear explanation is available. And whenever an answer is cobbled together, it disintegrates again in face of the actual experience, especially the experience of innocent suffering.

The focus of this chapter is on how Christianity interacts with the question and the mystery of suffering. I will not be arguing that Christianity has 'the answer'. But it does bring its own perspective to bear. It does throw light on the matter. It may even offer hope.

## *From suffering to God*

Suffering is everywhere. The senseless death of a child; the earthquake that wipes out a whole community. But also comes in less dramatic forms. A factory closes and jobs are lost; a life-changing injury; somebody unable to establish relationships; people who see no way out of their predicament. And so on. It would seem that to be is to suffer; it is that kind of existence. Even if we could eliminate the suffering caused by the violence of others, it would still be so.

So the question arises: 'Why me?' or 'Why this? Asking is not an intellectual exercise. The question is a cry, out of painful experience. It is formed and uttered out of agony, bewilderment, anger. It threatens to become despair.

It may become a question about life's meaning. Suffering is not evenly distributed. Some are lucky. Some people get more than their fair share. The poor, the 'little ones' of the earth, seem to get it worst. To add scandal to shock, the wicked, whose greed and hatred inflict so much suffering, are so often the ones who prosper.

That shakes our trust in things. We begin to wonder if the universe is in fact friendly and on our side. We wonder whether there is indeed a moral order to the universe. Perhaps the 'chaos' scientists speak of in the physical world is at the core of our human reality also. Perhaps it is just the way things are; no more to be said.

Yet, at the same time, a disturbing paradox is to be observed. Much of the time, suffering brings out the best in people. So often people's response is full of courage, endurance, solidarity, compassion. Regularly, suffering brings out such qualities in people. They are qualities that we might not otherwise discover, that would stay dormant were they not 'called forth' in this way.

This is not a rationale for suffering, simply a paradox stated. On the one hand, we have the absurdity and offensiveness of so much suffering. On the other, we note how it brings up depths of humanity in us. A world without suffering: what would it be like? What would we be like? We seem to touch here on something basic about our existence.

Finally, it becomes a question about God, at least for those who believe. For believers the question raised about God may be more disturbing than the question about suffering. How could God allow this to happen? What kind of God could that be? What could a good God possibly be up to? How could there be both God and such senseless suffering?

Since Auschwitz this question about God has become fundamental for theology. 'Theology' means discourse about God. But innocent suffering challenges the very validity of God talk. I recall somebody remarking that the only atheism to be taken seriously is the atheism which despairs at the absurdity of suffering.

### Which God?

It will help if we clarify which God we are talking about here. It is not some general idea of God. It is very specific: the God of Christians, the God of the Bible, the God of Jesus Christ. We are not speculating in the abstract as to how God might make sense of suffering. Rather, we are listening to a particular experience of God. We are listening to what Christians understand the God of Jesus Christ to do or say in the face of suffering.

The first impression I take from the Bible is that the question is bigger than the answers. There are different 'answers' to the mystery of suffering in the Bible. But it is the question that dominates and that reverberates persistently after all the answers are proposed – the question 'Why innocent suffering?' – the question about God.

As we read the Bible we are not looking up solutions. We are entering into a struggle with the problem. We meet people who are grappling and grieving. The psalms illustrate this. Of the 150 psalms, the great bulk are in the form, not of praise, nor of thanks, but of lamentation. The typical prayer to God is a cry out of suffering.

A feeling of confusion or perplexity characterises this prayer. On one side, there is awareness of the God of the Exodus, the liberating and compassionate God, the God 'for us'. 'Then they cried to the Lord in their trouble and he saved them from their distress' (Psalm 107:19). In contrast, there is also a distance, a strangeness, a silence to God. 'O Lord, how long will you look on?' 'Why do you hide your face from me?' (Psalms 35:17, 88:14).

*No answers*

The very strength of belief can, as it were, force through neat theories or answers or solutions to the dilemma. These then become the orthodoxy, the 'proper way to think'. One such theory that is prominent in the Bible is that suffering is the result of sin, a punishment. It goes along the lines of: 'If you are suffering, it cannot be God's fault, therefore you must have done something wrong.'

There are also the theories that suffering is a test from God, and that suffering is educative, character-forming. Such ideas are not confined to the Bible of course. But what the theories have in common is that they try to reduce everything to rational explanation. In the process they also make God understandable.

Suffering as punishment, as a test, as educative: all these contain some truth. But they are not enough, they are not satisfactory. Again and again, the personal experience of innocent suffering breaks through the orthodoxies and exposes the poverty of every rational solution. This is very evident in the character of Job, the quintessential good person who undergoes extreme and inexplicable suffering.

Job refuses to accept the traditional, orthodox answers. Not only does he reject the answers; he challenges God. If this is all there is to it, he insinuates, then God is cruel and arbitrary. He reverses the orthodoxy. Instead of saying that we suffer because we have sinned, he implies that it is God who has sinned in allowing us to suffer.

God does respond to Job; not quite an answer, not a solution to the problem, but a response. While questioning Job, God also commends him for 'speaking of God what is right' (42:7) – unlike his friends with all their 'answers'. This suggests that Job, by freeing the question from the grip of easy answers, has also freed God from rational reductions and released God back into mystery.

And that is where it rests. The mystery of innocent suffering persists, but it is somehow included within God's unfathomable designs. Job acknowledges that he has been speaking of things that he does not understand. But he also confesses that something has changed for him; 'I had heard of you by the hearing of the ear, but now my eye sees you' (42:5).

We are left with a sense of people holding on to the question, knowing no answer, maybe even resisting any answer. And we are left with a sense of people holding on to their God; not tying God down, or explaining God, but waiting on God. The two seem to merge. On the one hand, accepting that suffering has no answer. On the other, accepting the mystery that is God.

What comes across is that the suffering in our world is as much about the presence of God as it is about God's absence. Perhaps it is even more about God's presence. It seems that, faced with the unfathomable mystery of suffering, we are in the presence of the unfathomable mystery of God.

*The cross*

The cross is the great Christian symbol. Most immediately, it is a symbol of suffering. That suffering is articulated in Jesus' desolate cry on the cross: 'My God, my God, why have you forsaken me?' This says to us plainly that Christianity does not look on at suffering from a distance. It is bound up with suffering at its core. Christianity is rooted in Jesus; inside and not outside suffering, inside the pain, inhabiting it.

For Christians, Jesus' cry brings the whole experience of Jesus' people, already represented in Job, to a point. Like Job, Jesus is an innocent and good person. He was young, too young to die. He was an innocent victim of injustice. There is no hint that his suffering is in any way his punishment. (There are, however, those 'theories' we mentioned that misconstrue his death as a ransom, an atonement, a vicarious offering.)

Not only did Jesus suffer innocently. His whole life was a crusade against suffering. And his whole life sought to portray God's stance in the face of suffering. His life was a remarkable life of loving outreach to suffering humanity. In his own tears and compassion he felt the feelings and compassion of God.

Early Christianity's strong sense of this is reflected in how it interpreted his story of the Good Samaritan as being about him. He was divine passion and compassion incarnate. In the words of Augustine, the whole human race is the man lying on the road; and the Samaritan is Jesus, 'our near neighbour in mercy'.[14]

This was the person who suffered innocently and senselessly on the cross. And this background helps us appreciate how desolate and abandoned he felt as he uttered his final cry. So, when Christians proclaim that this Jesus is raised from the dead, what does that mean as regards suffering?

First, it takes us back to the thought above about the 'merging' of unfathomable suffering with the unfathomable God. If Jesus is raised, then the unfathomable mystery of God has appeared to us in the unfathomable mystery of suffering. In the words of Karl Rahner: 'The incomprehensibility of suffering is part of the incomprehensibility of God … Suffering is the form in which the incomprehensibility of God appears.'[15]

According to the Letter to the Hebrews, resurrection means that Jesus' cry was heard. 'Jesus offered up prayers and supplications, with loud cries and tears, to the one who was able to save him from death, and he was heard because of his reverent submission' (Hebrews 5:7). His suffering, both its trust and its desolation, was taken into God.

For Christians, this is not just saying something about Jesus. It is saying something about all suffering and it is saying something about God. The Christian view is that, in the cross of Jesus, all the suffering of humanity is gathered. He stands for all who have suffered, for all who do suffer, for all who will suffer innocently and needlessly. He stands for all who crusade against suffering, who share his compassion. All of it is equally heard and embraced and taken into God.

In the last chapter I offered a Christian perspective on evolution, where the mishaps and disasters of the process are somehow included within its larger purposes. Now it seems that

suffering too, in all its scandal and absurdity, may not be outside the scope of God's embrace, even if we do not see quite how
this is so.

In one sense, nothing has changed. Suffering goes on as before; it continues to perplex and affront us. 'God' remains unfathomable mystery. One thing, though, is new with Jesus. One
new thing has come onto the scene, and that is discipleship, the
following of Jesus. This is where the Christian attitude to suffering finally becomes clear.

## Discipleship

Christianity does not 'explain' suffering, except insofar as it
senses it to be embraced within the divine project of creation.
Rather than explain, it proposes a way of living through suffering, the way of discipleship. This way, however, has been reflected in different styles of spirituality.

One traditional spirituality talked about 'God's will'. When
our suffering stretches our capacity to accept, we 'offer it up' to
God. We 'carry our cross', we join our suffering to that of Jesus.
We trust in God's will even though we cannot grasp the reasons.
We take it on trust that it makes sense.

Sometimes linked with this is the view that this world is a
time and place of suffering. 'To suffer and endure is the lot of
humanity', as an old papal document put it.[16] In a similar vein,
the Hail Holy Queen prayer describes us as 'mourning and
weeping in this valley of tears'. It has been described as a spirituality of 'delayed gratification'; in this life we endure, in the
next life we will be comforted.

What do we make of this? On the plus side, there is its trust in
God, and the strength that comes from identifying with Jesus in
his suffering. Also, there is a realism about the hardships of life.
But on the minus side, there is a mood of resignation and passivity. This hardly reflects Jesus' proactive lifestyle in the face of suffering. It could even become compliance with the way things are.

Today, a different spirituality takes its cue from what the
theologian Johann Baptist Metz described as 'the dangerous
memory of the cross'.[17] To remember the cross is more than
being comforted in our faith. It is also dangerous, because of the
implications for how we live our lives. It is about activity, not
passivity. There are three moments in this remembering.

First, it looks to the past. This is the moment of faith. In remembering the cross we remember all who have suffered as Jesus did. As we do, we remember God. We believe that God hears their cries also, that all suffering is taken into God's compassionate heart. So, remembering the cross is already an act of solidarity with all of suffering humanity.

Second, it looks to the future. This is the moment of hope. Remembering is also an act of hope, hope that there is a future for all these, who would otherwise be forgotten. The Bible calls Jesus 'a forerunner on our behalf' (Hebrews 6:20). He is the 'anchor' for our hope that God will unveil a future beyond imagining for all of suffering humanity.

Third, remembering looks to the present. This is the moment when faith and hope translate into love. Faith and hope find expression in a solidarity with all who suffer, modelled on that of Jesus. This solidarity feels his divine compassion for people's pain. It feels his anger at the sin that causes so much suffering. It grows in commitment to a world transformed by right relations between people, relations built on solidarity and compassion.

This is the only Christian 'answer' to the question of suffering. It is not a theory, not an idea, but a way of living our lives. It is not an answer that is produced, but a hope that is lived. Christians live their 'way', not with the comfort or smugness of having worked it all out, but still waiting for God to fully appear.

While they follow Jesus, Christians still live 'on this side of the cross'. They live inside the desolation of the cry of the suffering: 'My God, why have you forsaken me?' But they do so with lives of solidarity and compassion. This is how they give witness to their hope and their faith.

I recall the paradox noted earlier, how suffering can bring out the best in people. Christian living immerses itself in that paradox, just as Jesus was immersed in it. In the face of suffering it mourns and it hopes and it responds. And it waits – for God.

*For reflection*
What do you think of the suggestion in this chapter that the suffering in our world is more about the presence of God than the absence of God?

CHAPTER SIXTEEN

## *Beyond this Life*

Recent times have seen quite a shift of emphasis in Catholic beliefs about the afterlife. Previously people were much more fearful of hell and much more anxious about their eternal salvation. Today there is more agnosticism, of course. But there is also a more confident tone among believers, a sense that we go straight to heaven. Perhaps it borders on presumption at times.

The shift is reflected in the funeral prayers for the deceased. There used to be a lot of emphasis on praying for the dead person, praying that God would forgive their sins. Now the prayers are more likely to be asking God to welcome them into their eternal home. They may even be thanking God for having so welcomed them.

Why the shift? It is not because we have acquired new information about the next life. It is that our convictions about the present have changed. We have changed in our sense of the God who is here and now. We have moved from a God of fear to a God of love.

This lies behind the welcome collapse of belief in 'limbo', that place where unbaptised infants supposedly went, that was neither heaven nor hell. The belief collapsed because we have come to believe in a God of love. We realise that such a God would not go on like that. Present experience and convictions shape future perspectives.

I am saying that there is a strong link between what we believe about the afterlife and what we believe in the present. The roots of Christian belief in the afterlife are in the present. It is not as if an explorer had returned with new information about uncharted territory. What we are experiencing now is the basis for all our thinking about then. What we say about the afterlife is the future dimension of our present experience of God.

### Already

This is the way the New Testament thinks. In the time after the resurrection there was a strong expectation of a second coming of Christ and, with it, of the end of the world. This expectation weakened over time, but very early on there emerged a sense of resurrection life as now.

This is very different from the dualism we have been accustomed to. By dualism I mean a sharp line between this world and the next, as two quite separate spheres of existence. New Testament reflection on the resurrection led, rather, to a strong sense of the next world as having 'broken through' into this one.

'If you have been raised with Christ, seek that things that are above; for you have died and your life is hidden with Christ in God' (Colossians 3:1-3). The language here is rooted in the baptism ceremony. Becoming a Christian is to have already entered into risen life. The imagery of 'hidden' suggests that what we call afterlife is both still to come and already mysteriously present.

The first letter of John puts it more directly. 'We know that we have passed from death to life because we love one another' (1 John 3:14). We have passed: Christian living has already begun to participate in another sphere of existence. The next life is, in a very real sense, now. The future has broken through into the present.

Something of this is reflected in the New Testament usage of the word 'saints'. For example, Paul's second letter to Corinth concludes: 'Greet one another with a holy kiss. All the saints greet you.' This refers, not to saints in heaven, but to Paul's companions, fellow Christians here on earth.

For us, saints are people who have been canonised, declared to be in heaven. For the early church, each Christian was a saint. Saint meant blessed, graced, holy. It meant that they were already participating in the life that is God's future for humanity. It was not so much that people had gone to heaven, as that heaven had come to people.

This links with the ancient idea that Christian living is a process of divinisation, of becoming divine. Our life is not merely a human life. It is living here a life divine. Faith in Christ is a belief that both divinity and humanity are in each one of us. Here, already, we are entering into our divinity. Our destiny of sharing in the trinitarian life of God has already begun to be realised.

*Echoes*
This is the distinctive perspective from which Christianity looks
at death and the afterlife. But it is not just meant for Christians.
Christianity sees this as the universal truth about humanity.
Indeed, there is something about it that echoes closely with our
deepest human experience, the experience of love.

The French philosopher Gabriel Marcel said somewhere
about love; 'To say "I love you" is to say "You, you in particular,
will never die".' We find a similar intuition in the Song of Songs
from the Bible: 'Love is strong as death ... many waters cannot
quench love, neither can floods drown it' (8:6-7).

There is something about the experience of love that touches
to eternity. It may be the experience of being in love; or family
love; or transcending the ego in other-centredness; or being
grasped by concern for a more just world. Whichever it may be,
love strives for eternity. It immortalises. To love, to be loved, is
to have glimpsed already what will be our eternal destiny.

Part of our intuition is that anything less would undo the
meaning we find in loving and being loved. This, our universal
experience, echoes the words above from John; when we love,
we have already passed from death to life. 'Love' here can be
taken to include all the dying-and-rising that happens in our
life, all our daily breaking through from death to life, from darkness to light, from despair to courage.

The good news of the gospel is its unveiling of this, the inner
truth of our human existence. It offers the assurance of what we
hope for, as it reveals the inner essence of love to be a participation in the divine. In our experience of love, our future is already
coming to pass. As we break through to new life, our future life
is breaking through into this one.

*Breaking through*
'Breakthrough' is the image I am using in talking about the New
Testament. It is the kind of imagery that captures the Christian
understanding of life, death and beyond. Life itself is characterised in terms of breakthrough to higher forms of being. And
death is the culminating breakthrough into the ultimate sphere
of existing.

Much of our imagining, however, has taken us in other

directions. Christians often think of the afterlife as a kind of resuscitation. We continue as we are, but in a different place. That is not the imagery and language of breakthrough. It carries little or no sense of transformation.

Again, Christians often think in terms of the immortality of the soul. In this life the soul is, as it were, trapped in the body. Death is its escape. This way of thinking comes from the influence of Greek rather than biblical ways of thinking. In the Bible, body and soul are not so distinct. Rather, we are each a unity, an embodied spirit, or a spiritual body.

The very word 'resurrection' suggests different imagery, very much along the lines of breaking through. It comprises both continuity and transformation. There is the same 'I' but in a new state and a new sphere of existence. We already saw this in the gospel accounts of the risen Jesus appearing to his disciples. He is the same, yet utterly different.

I think of Shakespeare's lines in *The Tempest* (the lines inscribed on Keat's tombstone in Rome): 'Nothing of him that doth fade/But doth suffer a sea-change/Into something rich and strange.'[18] For Christians, death is the person breaking through into a more fully spiritual mode of existence. It is not that life takes up from where it left off. It is not that the soul escapes from the body. It is an embodied spirit transformed, breaking through into fullness of being, into its fully spiritual self.

Another breakthrough image is the womb. Death-resurrection is parallel to birth from the womb into the world. Death is another birth, out of the womb of this world, into fullest reality. In each case there is the same incapacity for envisaging what life after the breakthrough is like. In each case there is identity and transformation, the same 'I' but a quite different 'I' – a different sphere of existing.

## Life beyond death

Unfortunately, our imagining of the afterlife has been dominated by the theme of judgment. After this life comes the reckoning, then the sentence; heaven or hell, eternal reward or eternal punishment. And our attention has focused more on punishment than on reward, more on hell than on heaven. We have taken literally the imagery ascribed to Jesus; as in the story of the rich man ('I am in agony in these flames' (Luke 16:24), or in the picturing of the final judgement ('Depart from me into the eternal fire', Matthew 25:41).

The graphic imagery may have the merit of asserting a moral order in life. But any merit is far outweighed by the image of God implied, a judgemental and punishing God. If we let go this theme of judgement, we can access a far more truthful picture of the God of Jesus Christ, a picture far more truthful to Jesus' own faith and imagination.

The fact is, we do not know what the afterlife is like. We have no pictures, no reports. What we do know is our faith, here and now, our convictions about God's eternal disposition towards us, as expressed in Jesus, his life, his actions and teachings, his dying and rising.

What we know is God's passion for us, God's outreach to us, God's self-sharing with us. We know this both as future promise and as present possession. Particularly in the love, compassion and solidarity amongst us, we know that we are already experiencing what we are going to be completely immersed in.

The next life is the completion of a dream and a promise that is already in the course of being realised. It is the fullness of life and love in the communion of Father, Son and Spirit. It is our present relationship with God surviving and enduring in a transformed state. Talk about the next life is not information about something of which we have no experience at all. It is the promise contained in what we already experience.

*Heaven*
We do not have detailed information about the next life, but we do have imagination. We can imagine our destiny on the basis of what we are already experiencing. And the adequacy of our images will be measured by how well they reflect what we know of God in this life. Here I offer some images from the Christian tradition for what people call 'heaven'.

We can take from the New Testament a triple imaging of heaven. It is the 'resurrection of the body': the individual's personal transformation. It is the 'kingdom of God': our communal transformation into the 'communion of saints'. And it is 'a new heaven and a new earth': the whole universe transformed, the ultimate or 'Omega' point in God's cosmic adventure.

This triple image corrects an individualistic tendency in our thinking about heaven. We have spoken of 'saving my soul', as if it were 'everybody for themselves'. We have seen heaven as me making it; and only incidentally you as well. But the afterlife is more than our personal rising to new life. It is also our solidarity as God's people. And it is in our solidarity with all God's creation, of which we are but the conscious moment.

The triple image also points to the next life, not just as our fulfilment, but as God's fulfilment. Whatever term we use – whether heaven or the kingdom or reign or rule of God – it all points to the afterlife as a state of affairs where what God wants has come to be, where God's wish holds sway. 'God reigns' in the sense that creation – God's dream, God's risk – has reached its goal.

Next, I want to bring together some images from Saint Augustine that give a flavour of the kind of thing heaven is. Sometimes we wonder what will everybody be doing in that life. And when we speak of it as 'eternal' life, it is hard to imagine how it will not at some stage or other become boring. These images bring it, I think, to a different level.

First Augustine presents the afterlife as a seeing. He talks of 'when we see that face'[19]: 'It is so lovely, so beautiful, that once you have seen it, nothing else can give you pleasure.' This echoes the Book of Sirach: 'Who could ever tire of beholding God's glory? (42:25). Traditionally this has been known as the 'beatific vision'.

The second image is that of a banquet. This image recurs in the gospels and is close to the heart of Jesus (eg Luke 14). As Augustine sees it, it will be a different kind of banquet. 'It will give insatiable satisfaction of which we will never tire; we shall always be hungry, always have our fill.'[20] There is the sense of our present experiences of longing and fulfilment being brought onto a new level of actualisation.

In a third image, that life will be praise. 'When we are finally home, praying will be out of place, there will only be praising. Why will praying be out of place? Because nothing will be lacking'.[21] In this life we sing God's praise; then we shall be God's praise.

In a fourth image, that life will be day. The word 'immortal' suggests endless time, stretching on forever. But it is more like an eternal now, a 'gathered time'. We only call it a day because that is what we are used to. But 'that day', says Augustine, 'knows no rising of the sun, knows no setting. That day is not followed by a tomorrow, because it is not preceded by a yesterday.'[22]

Finally he asks, how can something go on and on and not become boring? He tries to think of something in this life that does not at some point get boring. 'Yes, food can get boring, drink can get boring, entertainment can get boring ... good health, though, has never been found boring.'[23] The afterlife is like this well-being. It is pure actualisation in this sense, the pure pleasure and satisfaction of seeing and praising God.

## Hell and purgatory

I hinted above that we can move away from the language of judgement, or reward and punishment. God does not sit in judgement. God is simply eternal constant invitation into love. And God's invitation does not force itself upon us. Rather, it creates freedom, as our possibility of saying 'yes' to God. God's risk is our possibility. Our core identity is this potential for saying 'yes'.

As we know, our actual life history is never an unambiguous 'yes' or 'no'. Our life oscillates between the two, between entering into our humanity and failing to become. And in this life, our true self – that deepest core of what we truly are and truly feel – is inaccessible even to ourselves.

It would seem possible that a whole life story could amount to a 'no'. If we are truly free to decide for ourselves what to make of ourselves, then we are free to betray our humanity. If so, then what we call hell is at least a possibility. But this hell is not the punishment of a divine judge. It is self-chosen, self-inflicted. It is a no to self that is also a no to God. It is a no to others too, for full humanity lies in being-for-others.

This, though, does not mean that there is anybody in hell (even if the world is convinced that certain people must be). We can even say that Christians are called to hope that nobody is in hell. This goes hand in hand with hoping for the final triumph of good over evil. As we hear the cry of all the victims in humanity's story of injustice, we need not resort to believing in a God of retribution. We wait, rather, for the God of surprises.

This perspective makes purgatory a possibly more relevant idea than hell. We know that death takes us 'as we are'. When we die, our life is a now-finished and yet unfinished project. This suggests seeing our final assumption into God as a healing moment, a cleansing, a purification.

Early Christians proposed the image of restoring a flawed work of art to its original condition. Such healing, cleansing, restoring is what purgation means. It is not like a punishment before you are let out to play. It is not a transit station to decide if you go to heaven or to hell. But it is that the actual experience of entering into God is itself purgative.

*A prelude*
The mindset of judgement sees the relationship between this world and the next as 'if … then …' If we do good we are rewarded; if we do evil we are punished. It also implies that life here is a means to an end, doing what needs to be done in order to achieve the desired outcome, like studying for an exam. That is hardly the spirit of Christianity.

In contrast, the language of 'already and not yet' has a feel of entering into something. It suggests that what we have here in this life is a foretaste of what is hoped for, in which our ultimate future is already mysteriously present. The sense of expectation makes for a more, not less, intense living of this life.

Thus the composer Liszt offered this image of the relationship between this life and the next: 'What is our life but a series of preludes to that unknown song of which death sounds the first solemn and festive note?'[24] If our life is a prelude then the music has already begun. We are not doing a test and life is not an exam. We are responding to an invitation. The breaking through is already underway.

*For reflection*
Reflect on the imagery in this chapter for death and the afterlife. Which images speak most strongly to you?

CHAPTER SEVENTEEN

# Different Religions

This chapter is about one of the most debated topics in theology today. How does Christianity see itself in relation to other religions? I am thinking here of the great world religions, such as Judaism and Islam, Buddhism and Hinduism. But I am also thinking of the many other religious traditions around the globe, as well as the diverse expressions of spirituality today.

The book began with the idea that grace is universal. Then we went on to talk about the Christ event. But how do these connect? A dilemma presents itself here. How is it possible to assert both the status of the different religious traditions in the world and the uniqueness of what happened in the life, death and resurrection of Jesus?

On the one hand, people today have a new-found admiration for the religions of the world. As this respect increases, we tend towards thinking that all religions are of the same standing, as different paths to God and different expressions of the same human thrust towards the transcendent. We can end up thinking that it is just an accident of birth what religion a person professes, and that one religion is as good as another.

On the other hand, we have the perception within Christianity of its own decisive significance and unique position among the religions of the world. In Catholicism the sense of being the 'one true church' can appear arrogant. Thus a Vatican document from the year 2000 said that followers of other religions 'are in a gravely deficient situation in comparison with those who, in the church, have the fullness of the means of salvation'.[25]

How can we steer between the extremes of relativism and arrogance? How can we hold together a profound appreciation of all religions and an appreciation of the definitive nature of the Christ-event? Too much stress on the latter and other religions become inferior. Too much stress on the former and Christianity loses its uniqueness.

*A changing mindset*

Despite the document just quoted, the Catholic Church has travelled quite a distance in its attitude. In chapter two I referred to the view that held sway for so long: 'Outside the Church no salvation'. This implied that God favours those who have had the opportunity of joining the church and that countless millions through the centuries are denied God's grace. But the thinking represented in the documents of Vatican II is very different:

> Those who, through no fault of their own, do not know the gospel of Christ or his church, but who nevertheless seek God with a sincere heart and, moved by grace, try in their actions to do his will, as they know it through the dictates of their conscience; those also may achieve eternal salvation. Nor shall divine providence deny the assistance necessary for salvation to those who, without any fault of theirs, have not yet arrived at an explicit knowledge of God and who, not without grace, strive to live a good life.[26]

It is clear in this that grace is universally available and that believing in Christ is not necessary for salvation. One renowned theologian, Karl Rahner, coined the phrase 'anonymous Christianity' to speak of this. The idea of somebody being an anonymous Christian has patronising overtones and received a mixed reception. But the intention was otherwise. Rahner was not trying to 'corral' non-Christians. He was pointing to the breadth of God's vision and to the narrowness of church and religion.

The idea is that God reaches out to all humanity without exception and that all can access God through the authenticity of their living. If God's outreach comes to full expression in Christ, that does not make the situation of non-Christians inferior. The response contained in their living is just as valid as that of Christians, even if they do not perceive their living as a 'response'. Thus their response is called anonymous Christianity.

What is happening here is the move from a church-centred to a Christ-centred mindset. Salvation is not centred on the church and on membership of the church. It is centred on Christ and what God offers in Christ is universally available. But, while this is certainly a more generous stance, does it go far enough? Is it still giving Christianity a prominence that effectively down-grades other religions?

One theologian put it like this; are members of other religions saved despite their religious traditions or because of them? The description of other religions being in a 'gravely deficient situation' is 'despite' thinking. It implies that other religions are like a series of unfortunate historical aberrations. It suggests that God manages to rescue people nonetheless, through a kind of universal effect of the Christ-event.

'Because' thinking paints a different picture. Here we can think of different religions each being a path to God in its own right. In that case they are very relevant. They are integral to God's outreach to humanity. With this thought we are not just moving from a church-centred to a Christ-centred view. We are also broadening our perspective to a God-centred mindset.

### God-centred

'Because' thinking says that God's designs are in a sense bigger than the Christ-event. God's outreach may have come to its fullest realisation in Christ, but Christ and Christianity are not the whole story. The history of religions is all of it embraced in God's vision. The variety of religious traditions is blessed by God. God rejoices in the diversity of religions.

We are trying here to hold together two things. One is that the different religions are part of God's vision and that, in and through their different religions, people can find all that God is and means. The other is that Christ is the decisive moment in God's creative presence in the world.

As a way of illustrating this, think of a flash of lightning over a dark countryside. The lightning does not add anything new to the landscape, but it lights up everything. In a similar way, the Christ-event is called God's definitive 'revelation'. It is the complete revelation of God's intentions in creation and God's vision for the world. To refer to an earlier chapter, it is not the added extra something of 'Plan B' thinking. It is the original 'Plan A' in its full dimensions.

Thomas Merton once quoted a question asked by Gandhi: 'How can he who thinks he possesses absolute truth be fraternal?'[27] The truth is bigger than all of us; we do not possess it, but together we participate in it. In the same way Christianity does not possess the truth or possess salvation. It is not that salvation arrives with Christianity. The world is where salvation is happening, where grace is experienced and lived in saving ways among people, however they may name it.

But Christianity is the place of revelation. It is where this comes to a point of articulation, where it is given a name and disclosed for what it is. As somebody put it: the world is the place of salvation and Christianity is the place of revelation. In that sense it is the defining moment in God's outreach to humanity. In this spirit arrogance gives way to humility; a humble and appreciative wonder at all that God is doing.

This may well have been the original spirit of Christianity. The first disciples were Jews who, painfully, came to see that the resurrection expressed God's intentions for all people. It marked the end of thinking in terms of a 'chosen people', because all are chosen. The Spirit of God is a boundary-breaking Spirit.

In the end, what is necessary for salvation to happen is not baptism, or church membership, or being Christian. What is necessary is God: God who is reaching into creation as Spirit, who is giving God's self as Christ. This cannot be separated up into different 'givings' a better one for Christianity, a lesser one for everybody else. It is the one God throughout, the one gift, the one vision.

*Sacraments*

What about baptism, then, and sacraments generally? If salvation does not depend on being baptised, then what is happening when a person is baptised? If God's saving presence is available universally, what is going on in the sacraments? Here too there is a change of mindset needed.

We are conditioned to think that sacraments are about receiving something or having something done to us. Notice the language we use, especially the word 'get'. I get baptised; I get confirmed; I get anointed; I get confession; I get Mass; I get communion. Sacraments are seen as transactions between an individual and God, where we are passive, where we are acted upon, and where we get something called 'grace'.

But in the perspective of this chapter, grace is already there, universally available. What is going on in the sacraments is that

we are celebrating this. Sacraments are special moments of
heightened awareness and heightened receptivity. We still 'get'
something, but we see it and express it differently.

Thus baptism is not adequately described as cleansing a person of original sin. The Christian view is that everybody comes
into the world already graced. Baptism is a celebration of the
grace that is already there. It does not make the person graced,
so much as rejoice that they are graced. And it rejoices in Christ,
in whom God's gracing of humanity is accomplished.

In this, baptism is also the person's entry into the community
of Christians. It initiates an individual into the community that
shares this revelation as its cause for rejoicing and the focus of
its unity. Christianity is about a community of revelation and
celebration. It is not a community that feels superior. It is a community that feels blessed with a revelation into the truth about
all humanity.

Baptism is the entry sacrament in this sense, but Eucharist is
the central sacrament of the community. The word means
'thanksgiving'. Eucharist is sacrament, not primarily in the
sense of getting something, but in the sense of celebrating something, of rejoicing, of giving thanks. This is powerfully symbol-
ised by the story of the ten lepers whom Jesus healed (Luke
17:11-19).

The ten stand for humanity. All were in the same situation of
being graced and experiencing grace. But one returned to Jesus
to say thanks. One of them had a sense of the source of the grace.
He stands for Christianity. He knows something, but it is something that concerns everybody. He is not more graced than the
others, but he is in a place of revelation.

The people who gather to offer thanks share a profound
sense of revelation. They appreciate that, in Jesus, the full dimensions of God's intentions for all humanity are realised. But
their thanks is not simply for what they themselves have received. It is more humble and gracious than that. It is thanks for
God's gracing of all humanity. It is a universal rejoicing.

*Dialogue*
Thinking today has moved beyond converting people to the
church. More and more it is felt that the good news of the gospel
is best heard in a context of dialogue rather than proselytising,

of listening as well as speaking. This is the new face of what Christians call 'evangelisation' or 'mission'.

Dialogue between Christianity and other religions is more than 'you join us'. That is church-centred; it sees the point of unity to be where we are at. In today's style of dialogue, the point of unity is outside all of us, beyond all of us. The dialogue is God-centred. Here, the truth is not something any of us possess. It is a point we can all converge upon.

Actual dialogue between religions takes a number of forms. There is a dialogue of life, about getting to know and trust each other. There is a dialogue of action, about working together on shared values. There is theological dialogue, about understanding each other's beliefs and worldview. There is a dialogue of religious experience, about entering into prayer together.

What is crucial is the spirit of dialogue. The spirit is that each of us and each of our traditions are held in God's embrace. It is that the same God is present in all our perceptions of God. It is that we cannot arrive at so great a mystery as God by one and the same path. The God we share is ever beyond the grasp of any of us, but we can arrive closer when our paths converge.

Dialogue like this does not dilute conviction. If anything it is the opposite; we understand ourselves better when we understand one another. As in a phrase I heard somewhere: 'without difference no perception.' We open ourselves to the other, to what is different. We leave behind all thoughts of winning over, all thoughts of what they need to learn from us. Then we can emerge enlightened, even evangelised. So the two grow together; our commitment to our own faith and our openness to others.

I have not spoken about the differences and the different traditions within Christianity. But the same spirit applies there also. Christians can learn to think less about their different churches and what divides them. They can learn to share more about the Christ they all believe in. They can come to see their different traditions as being embraced in God's vision. They can welcome the enrichment of diversity.

*For reflection*
The different religions are part of God's vision and Christ is the decisive moment. What would be your way of explaining how these two statements hold together?

CHAPTER EIGHTEEN

# Women and Christianity

What are Catholics to make of their church's position on women? That church proclaims the radical equality of all people in God's eyes. Yet women cannot be ordained priests, which also excludes them from decision-making and power. It is maintained that this is quite coherent; women, it is argued, are 'equal but different'. But most people now see it as contradictory; equal in theory, but effectively unequal. For many, it means that the church is deeply male-centred and patriarchal.

*The argument*
The reason given for the church's position is that this was the intention of Jesus. He chose twelve apostles and they were all men. This was a deliberate choice, not his buying into the patriarchal mentality of the time. If this is the case, then the church sees itself as having no authority to change it.

At the Last Supper, the argument continues, Jesus instituted the Eucharist and the priesthood. When he said: 'Do this in memory of me', he entrusted its celebration to these men. Thus the priest who celebrates the Eucharist was to be a man. As it is put in the letter to the Ephesians (chapter five), this symbolises the relationship between Christ as 'bridegroom' (i.e. a male) and the church as 'bride'.

The suggestion here is of a deep theological truth. It is intended by God that Jesus be male and so a male priesthood is also God's plan. Only a male can represent Christ in his relationship to the church as bridegroom to bride. It is nothing to do with cultural conditioning; it is divinely decreed.

That makes it a very big issue. It is not a surface matter of simply changing a convention that excludes women from priesthood. It is much more systemic. It is written into the pages of scripture. It is inseparable from the way we understand God and understand humanity.

But today, all this is to be seen in the context of the rise of feminist consciousness. Feminism is a consciousness regarding the fact of sexual oppression in our world. It sees patriarchy as the root of this oppression. Patriarchy means a world centred on men and ruled by men, where men's ways of thinking and being are the norm.

From this point of view, the Christian God depicted above is part of the problem. 'He' is a patriarchal and oppressive God, not a true God. If the Bible is 'the word of God', then it is God's authoritative statement of God's own patriarchal nature. And his Jesus cannot be Messiah, at least not for half of the human race. This makes the gender question perhaps an even bigger issue than that of the relationship between Christianity and other religions.

### Jesus and women
Contemporary scholarship challenges our perspectives on the Bible. It has shown us, incontrovertibly, that women have a prominence in the gospels that is in stark contrast with Jewish culture of the time. But the texts have been submerged, as it were. It is only in the context of today's feminist consciousness that they surface again.

When Jesus calls Peter, Andrew, James and John, they leave their fishing nets to follow him, to 'fish for people' (Matthew 4:18-22). That much is familiar. But when he encounters the Samaritan women drawing water (Jn 4), she leaves her water jars, becomes his disciple, and 'draws' others to him to. This is unprecedented. But why has it passed us by? Why do we remember only the men?

Again, in Matthew's gospel, Peter confesses: 'You are the Messiah, the son of the living God' (16:16). But when Jesus visits Bethany, Martha says to him: 'You are the Messiah, the son of God, the one coming into the world' (John 11:27). Peter's confession has become foundational for the church. Martha's has been forgotten. Again, it is something unprecedented, and it has been submerged.

There are other examples. There is the Syro-Phoenician woman who opens Jesus' mind to the Gentiles (Mark 7). There is the woman who ministers to Jesus, anointing his feet (Luke 7). There are the women who are part of his inner circle (Luke 8). And after his death, when the twelve apostles have run away, women are the first to the tomb, the first to encounter him risen, the first to announce the news.

Jesus belongs in the tradition of the prophets. The prophets, such as Amos and Jeremiah, are the Bible's inner voice of self-criticism. They confront the existing order with the truth of what it is meant to be. They see where the relationship between God and God's people goes off course. They critique how God's people have become 'like the nations', taking on the trappings of power and hierarchy and oppression.

Continuing in this tradition, the main theme of Jesus' life was the reign of God. It is about a situation of right relationships among all God's people. It means a God of the poor and oppressed, liberator of the excluded, defender of the weak. If this is Jesus' God, it is to be expected that expectations will be upturned when Jesus is around. We can now see how this was happening in the case of women too.

What is happening for us is that we are now reading the Bible 'contextually'. We are reading it from our own context, with our own questions and concerns. These include the questions and concerns of feminism. Reading is now two-way. What we bring to the reading releases the text, allows it to reveal itself in new ways. That makes the text alive, capable of becoming a new word in a new situation, while still remaining the same word.

When the gospels are read contextually, submerged texts come to the surface again. In our case, texts re-surface that cast women in a different light. The texts were always there but we could not see them, because of where we were coming from. But when we do see them, we are led to think that, possibly, patriarchy is not necessarily part of 'the word of God'.

*An alternative reading*
So we can take a new look at some of the difficult issues from this angle. I am thinking of how Jesus addressed God as his 'father' and of how the disciples came to see him as the 'son' of God. I am thinking of his choosing twelve men as his inner circle of followers.

Jesus did address God as 'father', but there is nothing to suggest that he was thinking of the patriarchal God, and much to suggest the opposite. He says, 'Call no one your father on earth, for you have one Father, the one in heaven' (Matthew 23:9). This God has nothing to do with hierarchies of power. Jesus' God is a

God of radical equality among all God's people. There is to be no 'lording it' over one another, just as there is no such lording on the part of God (Matthew 20:25-28).

He may have called this God 'father', but his God is as much 'mother' as 'father'. Think of the words of Isaiah; 'Can a woman forget her nursing child, or show no compassion for the child of her womb? Even these may forget, yet I will not forget you' (49:15). We do not find these words on the lips of Jesus, yet they capture very precisely the spirit of what he was about. Indeed, is there any more powerful image than this for his God?

What then of Jesus being called 'son' of God? When the disciples proclaimed his resurrection, the symbol of son came to the fore. However, its main intent is the symbolic one of saying that Jesus is 'of God', just as children are 'of' their parents. Its concern is not about gender, but about what I earlier called the 'God-side' of Jesus.

Here it is worth noting that the New Testament also speaks of this 'God-side' in a feminine way. When John's gospel says that the Word became flesh (1:14), it is the Old Testament Wisdom tradition that is in the background. 'Wisdom' is a personification of God, now identified with Jesus. And the word is feminine. Likewise the word 'Spirit' in the Old Testament is feminine; the Spirit-God that filled Jesus from birth to death and beyond.

If Jesus is God's 'self-portrait', it can hardly be argued that the self-portrait necessarily had to be male, or that God intended that it should be male as opposed to female. Given the cultural context, it is hard to imagine that this figure would not have been male. But that is culture and not theology. The theological indications are in another direction. The God portrayed in Jesus is a boundary-breaking God.

What about his choosing twelve men? When he chose twelve men, we have no access to any intentions of Jesus regarding gender. The 'twelve' was a reference to the twelve tribes of Israel. In that number he was symbolising his dream of a new Israel. He was not setting up ecclesiastical structures. That the twelve were male most likely reflects how Jesus was embedded in the culture of his time. There is nothing to indicate that gender had any more significance than that.

*Tradition*

In its earliest days, Christianity was not so much a church in our sense as a spirit-inspired movement. The movement was counter-cultural. This is reflected in its strongly pacifist stance. It is reflected in an incipient distancing from slavery. And it is reflected in a re-configuration of male-female. Women are co-workers in spreading the gospel. Women are leaders of house churches.

As the movement grew into a church, it gradually lost its counter-cultural stance. Compare these texts from Paul. He writes to the Galatians: 'There is no longer Jew or Greek, there is no longer slave or free, there is no longer male and female; for all of you are one in Christ Jesus' (3:28). Not long after, he writes to Corinth: 'For in the one Spirit we were all baptised into one body – Jews or Greeks, slaves or free' (1 Corinthians 12:13). Where has the 'male and female' gone?

In Corinth, Christianity encountered the Greco-Roman world 'head-on'. Comparing the two texts, we are led to imagine a moment when Christianity compromised in order to survive. That would be consistent with the overall developments. Women soon disappeared from ministry. Later, in a parallel development, pacifism would give way to the theory of the just war.

As Christianity changed from being persecuted to being the official religion of the Empire, it took on many of the trappings of power and hierarchy and patriarchy. We inherit that tradition. And so, when we think of women in the New Testament, we are likely to think of 'wives be subject to your husbands' (Ephesians 5:22); or 'women should be silent in the churches' (1 Corinthians 14:34). The other texts have been submerged, they have vanished out of sight.

Over the centuries, men's ways of thinking became the norm. Theology came to define women as subordinate, as inferior beings. They were seen as more responsible then men for 'original sin'. Dichotomies grew up between male and female. On one side there is God (male), on the other world (female). On one side there is the spiritual (male), on the other the bodily (female). One was active, the other passive; one was to be obeyed, the other to obey.

In such a tradition, only the male can represent God. God becomes male and becomes, in the process, a ruler, a judge, powerful, even violent. Jesus too is necessarily male. A male priesthood and hierarchy is divinely ordained. When John Paul II defends the latter, one of his arguments is the constant practice of the church. But what looks more likely to be the case is that this constant practice is itself the legacy of patriarchy.

Matthew's gospel tells of an encounter between Jesus and the Pharisees. They ask him: 'Why do your disciples break the tradition of the elders?' And he answers: 'Why do you break the commandment of God for the sake of your tradition?' (15:1-3). Jesus' words throw light on what happened subsequently among his followers

Jesus criticised his religion for making God secondary to the traditions. There is a strong sense emerging from our discussion that the same has been happening since, that traditions have been elevated to the status of divine truth. The God of Jesus Christ, I would suggest, is more like one who subverts our human traditions and breaks the boundaries of what we think possible.

Sometimes, in a difficult situation, people ask; what would Jesus do? If Jesus were walking the earth today, choosing his 'twelve apostles', would all of them be men? And would there be only men at his 'last supper'? It is very hard to imagine 'yes' as the answer. What is that telling us? I do not think it is saying that our tradition is beyond redemption. Rather, our contemporary experience is inviting us into a new chapter in the appreciation of our religion, a new moment in our tradition.

*Mary*

How does Catholic devotion around Mary, mother of Jesus, sit with all this? On one hand it is said that her prominence is a strong affirmation of women. On the other, it is argued that the cult of Our Lady contributes to the downgrading of women in the church. Perhaps there is truth in both, but it is also true to say that the cult leaves the male God unchallenged.

The gospels offer a helpful approach. When somebody said to Jesus: 'Blessed is the womb that bore you', he replied: 'Blessed rather are those who hear the word of God' (Luke 11:27-28). And again, when told that his family were looking for him, he replied: 'Whoever does the will of God is my brother and sister and mother' (Mark 3:35). This is how Augustine related these sayings to Mary:

It means more for Mary to have been a disciple of Christ
than to have been the mother of Christ ... That is why
Mary is blessed, because she heard the word of God and
kept it. She kept truth safe in her mind even better than
she kept flesh safe in her womb ... So then, look to yourselves ... Take thought to how you can be what he said:
'Look, there are my mother and my brothers.' How are
you to be Christ's mother? And whoever hears, and
whoever does the will of my Father, that person is a
brother, a sister and a mother to me.[28]

The passage is thought-provoking It presents Mary as our fellow disciple. It invites us to see her as our sister; at least as much
a sister as a mother to us. This also implies a kind of working
principle: that whatever we say of Mary can in some way also be
said about ourselves.

Obviously, if we talk of Mary carrying Jesus in her womb,
that is unique. But if we talk of her as Augustine does, then we
can identify with her. So we too can be 'mothers of Christ'. This
gives us a way of spiritually interpreting her being mother and
virgin. When God's Spirit 'conspires' with our spirit, then we
give birth to Christ in our soul. That is our annunciation, our
incarnation.

Likewise we can relate what the church calls her 'immaculate
conception' to ourselves. That doctrine says she was free from
all 'stain' of original sin. Applying it to ourselves, we recall what
was said earlier about original sin and original grace. Then it
stands for the truth that all of us are born into grace, that all of us
are born 'full of grace'.

And we can see ourselves in what the church says about her
'assumption' into heaven. The truth of this for us is about our
life as a process of becoming divine, of being assumed into and
growing into the Trinitarian life of God. In all these instances we
are putting the focus on what we can relate to. Then we see that
we are sisters and brothers with Mary – in discipleship.

*For reflection*
What do you think is the most convincing argument in favour of
women priests? What do you think is the most convincing argument against women priests?

CHAPTER NINETEEN

# Christianity and Morality

The focus of this chapter is the question, what does Christianity have to say about morality? By morality I mean morality in general. I will not be talking about specific moral issues. I will be investigating the stance of Christianity with regard to morality as such; where morality fits into the overall scheme of Christian faith.

Some people will react that Christianity (at least in its Catholic version) is concerned with nothing else but morality. In Ireland, as elsewhere, religion and morality have become very tangled up in each other. Religion has spent a lot of its time talking about morality, so much so that people came to think that religion is where morality comes from. This also led to the widespread impression that the morality is the religion.

We can see where this leads when people disengage from the church over a moral issue. They cannot in conscience go along with the church position on an issue or a range of issues. They feel that, to preserve integrity, they have to walk away. They have been given the impression that conformity on some specific moral issues is a precondition for continuing to belong.

The approach in this chapter is to separate Christianity and morality from one another. First, we will see that morality is an independent matter, that it stands on its own two feet. Second, we will see that Christianity's primary focus is something other than morality. Third, then, we will see how Christianity links in with our moral living.

## Morality
If asked where to go to find the content of Christian morality, many would say 'the ten commandments'. It is an odd answer, given that the ten commandments are an expression of Jewish morality. They predate Christianity by many centuries and have no reference to Christ. Even more than that; they (the specifically moral injunctions, that is) predate Jewish morality also.

We have a picture of Moses descending the mountain, with the commandments written on tablets of stone. The impression is of a revelation newly received. But we need to ask ourselves: is this, somewhere in the thirteenth century before Christ, when it was first revealed that we should not kill or steal or betray? What was the situation for previous generations?

Whatever happened on the mountain, it was not that. We know from archaeology that neighbouring societies and civilisations of the ancient Near East had similar moral codes. Those codes are not privileged revelations from on high. The point is captured by Paul in his letter to the Romans. 'When Gentiles, who do not possess the (Jewish) law, do instinctively what the law requires ... they show that what the law requires in written on their hearts' (2:14-15). Morality is within.

Religion is not the source of morality. It is not where knowledge of right and wrong comes from. Morality is independent of religion. If not, that would imply partiality on God's part. God would be privileging some people over others by revealing 'the way' to them. (It would also mean that things are right or wrong because God said so, rather than because of some rationally accessible reason.)

So, morality is not religious in that sense. But it is very spiritual. It goes much deeper than rules and conformity to rules. Ultimately morality is about the other. It is about our responsiveness to one another as human persons. This responsiveness is nurtured from a sense of awe and reverence at the dignity and value of each other person.

Someone asked, why should we treat other people well? The reply came: because we are other people! Moral rules are nothing other than formulations of some of the demands of our interrelatedness. Also, if we are 'other people', this morality includes treating ourselves with the same respect that others deserve from us.

This means that what we call self-fulfilment is not something narcissistic. Rather, it is the by-product of following through on this 'otherness'. The two go together, other-centred living and discovering the deepest in ourselves. Becoming our best selves does not come from focusing on ourselves. It comes from commitment to the truth that we are all 'other people'.

There is something very spiritual about that. But it is essentially a human thing, in the sense that it is common to us all. It is not based in religion, but in our sense of who we are and who we are called to be.

People may disagree with this view. One objection says that we are fundamentally self-interested rather than other-centred. Another says that there is no such thing as objective morality, there are just our feelings: 'What's right for me'. Another says that what we call morality is just the conventions and laws of a particular society.

The view here is that the fact of our common humanity invites us to a shared perception of what being a human being is all about. I am saying that our humanity is a 'call' to become more human, to become our best selves. And I am saying that this happens in response to the demands of inter-relatedness.

Even were this much agreed, we would still disagree about what to do in different situations. For instance, somebody is caring for an elderly parent who is suffering greatly with no hope of recovery. Could euthanasia ever be the best response in such a situation? There is no way of eliminating differences of judgement here, unless we want to force everybody to think the same way.

Nevertheless, the capacity is in us, to reflect on our experience of living this human life. The capacity is in us to come to feel the call of the other, and to refine our feelings according to this truth. The capacity is in us to engage with different views of what the call concretely demands of us.

*Christianity*

This is the first point, that morality is independent of religion. The second point is that Christianity is not primarily about morality, despite appearances to the contrary. This realisation has been growing in recent decades within Catholicism. And when religion and morality are separated from one another, the separation allows Christianity to re-connect with its own true identity.

Of course, Christianity has things to say about how human beings live their lives in the world. But the first thing it has to say is not about what we do at all. The first thing is about what God does. The heart of Christianity is its proclamation about what God has done in the life, death and resurrection of Jesus. Its essence is good news for humanity.

Christianity is God-talk, Christ-talk, not rules-talk. It talks about the God 'portrayed' and embodied in Jesus, the God of compassion and solidarity. It talks about our destiny as it is revealed in Jesus. That destiny is about entering into our divinity, into participation in God. And that destiny is hope for the forgotten, the victims, God's 'little ones'.

The first letter of John reads: 'In this is love, not that we loved God but that God loved us' (4:10). That is the sequence for our thinking. So Christianity has the character of 'invitation and response'. In a sense it does not ask us to do anything at all. It comes to us as gift. It asks us to allow God to do something. It invites us to allow ourselves to be loved

## Christianity and morality

We can now begin to see some of the ways this connects with our moral living. I said that morality is independent and that figuring it out is within our grasp. But there are also questions which it cannot answer.

Our moral sense can tell us what is right or wrong. But it cannot tell us where it is all going. Is this moral impulse in us just some blind evolutionary spark? Is the universe, in the end, friendly to the moral task? We commit ourselves deeply to moral values. That prompts us to think there is something enduring here. It prompts us to hope. But is that prompting a false promise? We cannot say.

Likewise, our moral sense is helpless before the contradictions it comes up against. Good and innocent people suffer. So often it is the wicked who prosper. Life as we know it is not fair. But is that the ultimate state of affairs? Is there justice when all is said and done? And, in relation to our own experience of guilt, is there ultimate forgiveness? We cannot say.

We cannot say because such questions bring us beyond morality. They are religious or theological questions, whatever their answer may be. It is here, at this level, that Christianity mainly connects with our moral striving, rather than at the level of what to do. Its good news is a statement about the overall shape of things. As such it can speak into our moral experience in a helpful, hopeful way.

Christianity affirms and confirms our moral instinct, especially the instinct to other-centred, value-inspired living. It sets our moral living in the context of our ultimate destiny. It reveals the inner essence of our moral living. That essence is not that we live good lives in order to go to heaven. It is that our moral living is already grace, already an experience of our eternal destiny.

*Discipleship*

I am saying that Christianity offers a context for our morality. It articulates a context that confirms our hope and strengthens our motivation. But does it offer content as well as context? Does it have anything more specific to say about how we live our lives? Is there a Christian morality?

There is a Christian morality; but not in the sense of a set of rules for behaviour. The Catholic tradition has been quite immersed in formulating such rules. It was so immersed that it lost sight of what Christian morality is. For many centuries, books of Catholic morality were notable for the lack of any sense of Christian spirituality.

Christian morality is not rules, but relationship. It is about discipleship, a relationship with Jesus Christ. Discipleship does not change the demands of moral living. Those demands, as we have said, are independent. But following Jesus sets moral living in a new key. It is experienced differently.

What does that mean? First, it means that living is imbued with the mood of the gospel, the mood of good news, the mood of Jesus' life and teaching. It is imbued with a mood of gratitude for the grace of life and its Giver. It is imbued with a mood of hope, that living has such purpose and direction. It is imbued with a mood of vigilance, alive to the many possibilities of being surprised by grace.

Second, it means that the values of other-centred living are 'charged' with the passion of Jesus' own living. The commitment to compassion and solidarity is accentuated, especially solidarity with the poorest. There is a strong sense of the power of forgiveness and the power of non-violence as the way of human relationships. All of this generates its own criterion of what counts as 'success' in human and social living.

For this to come about, Christians have to work at it. They have to enter into the mindset of the gospels, they have to learn the mindset of Jesus. As Paul puts it, 'Let the same mind be in you that was in Christ Jesus' (Philippians 2:5). They have to allow themselves to be formed by his values and priorities. As they do, they discover that they are also entering more fully into their own humanity.

### Church

Christian morality is about discipleship. But discipleship is not a solitary life. It is about participating in the community of disciples called church. That community is also a community of discernment. In it Christians seek to discern with each other how to live life in the world, faithful to what their faith has revealed to them about life in the world.

This is meant to be a creative experience. The Bible is not a rulebook to be consulted for answers to moral dilemmas. Many of the issues facing us did not exist in those times, or are understood quite differently. Many of the moral directives in the Bible are culturally conditioned. What the Bible does offer is vision and values, priorities and principles. But we ourselves have to make the connections to our lives today.

Nor is the church meant to be a kind of book of rules, though it allowed itself to become that. It is meant to keep the vision alive. It is meant to encourage freedom and responsibility, creative and conscientious discipleship rather than mindless obedience. It is meant to encourage dialogue and the development of the collective wisdom. It is meant to move beyond a culture of control to a culture of ownership.

### For reflection

What kind of influence, both positive and negative, has Christianity had on your approach to morality?

CHAPTER TWENTY

## *Called by Name*

With this chapter we move into the third section of the book. The focus now is on everyday Christian living. I begin with something that all Christians have in common, be they married or single, men or women, young or old, rich or poor. That something is their shared identity and it puts them all on an equal footing, whatever positions they may occupy in the church. I am taking the old word 'vocation' as a way into articulating what this basic Christian identity is.

### Vocation

Vocation usually means a divine call to some occupation. In days past it had a broader reference than it has now. For instance, nurses, civil servants, teachers would have seen their work as a calling. We had 'vocational schools'. But that is all passed; now the work is simply a job or a profession (which, oddly, is another religious word).

Now the idea of a vocation is confined to religious and priests. And these callings have come to be seen as both rare and strange. Somebody 'getting a call' conjures up an odd experience – like being in a room with the window open, and the wind blows, and something happens … It is like what is depicted in paintings such as those of Botticelli or Fra Angelico of the angel's annunciation to Mary.

There is also a sense of being trapped. When God calls somebody it can seem that there is no choice. They have to obey. Yet it also seems to be just a few poor unfortunates that are called. Most people escape; God leaves them alone. The wise option would be to stay out of the way of such a call, so as to live life in peace.

I want to broaden the use of the word, to get it into a more ordinary space, where people can see themselves in it. I want to propose that the vocation or call is to Christianity, and not to priesthood or religious life. In other words, being a Christian is itself the calling. The calling is shared by all. It is both ordinary and special.

But before going into that, I would add a qualification. I do not wish to suggest that only Christians are called by God. Christianity is a calling for all Christians, but there is something more basic, shared by all human beings. It is this: to be a human being is the most fundamental vocation of all. How could somebody be a human being and not be called?

To each person God says: 'I have called you by name; you are mine' (Isaiah 43:1). Indeed, a little later in Isaiah, the words are addressed, not to any of the Jews (the 'chosen' people), but to the Persian Cyrus (45:4). The call is universal. God has called each and every one of us into being. Once born, God forever calls us forth into fuller being, to experience more fully what it is to be a human being.

### Beloved

To understand what it means to be called as a Christian, the first step is to understand baptism. And to understand baptism we need to put it in the present tense. It is more than something that had to be done in the dim and distant past, like a childhood inoculation. It is about more than original sin; once done, then forgotten.

Baptism is about original blessing more than original sin. It is about who we are in God's eyes, not back then but now. Pope John Paul II expressed it in the following way:

> Rising from the waters of the baptismal font, every Christian hears again the voice that was once heard on the banks of the Jordan river: 'You are my beloved'.[29]

Baptism celebrates the good news that at the core of our being we are 'beloved', blessed, just as Jesus is. One theologian even asked: 'Do you believe that the Father loved Jesus more than he loves you? Anyone who believes this does not seem to have heard the good news.'[30] Put another way: they have not grasped their own baptism.

This is the first meaning of being called. We are called to hear the good news and to experience it in our life. We are called to rejoice that we are beloved, that our life is graced, that life has eternal meaning. We are called to enjoy living our life because this is what we are. Our living is to be suffused with gratitude and appreciation, as we allow ourselves to be loved.

This is a powerful base from which to live life. Life itself may be lucky or unlucky, tranquil or stormy, cruel or kind. There are different ways that people handle that. But Christians can deal with their life experience from this base. They have this sense of being blessed and beloved. With this sense they are disposed towards finding grace in life's various ups and downs.

*Together*
The second aspect of vocation: Christianity is a call to togetherness. This is a crucial point because it is so overlooked. More often than not the word 'vocation' suggests something individual, something between the individual and God. Even the phrase 'being a Christian' can have a very individual, almost private ring to it. This seriously distorts the meaning of the Christian calling.

Christianity is a together thing. In the chapter on church I spoke about the original meaning of the word in the New Testament. It meant, not a building or an institution, but a gathering. It meant the people who assembled in this place for the breaking of bread. I said that another translation of the word is 'convocation', which is made up of the prefix 'with and 'vocation'.

This invites us to think of vocation as a 'with' word. Vocation may be very personal but it is not private. It was never meant to be just some mysterious individual experience. It is a call to togetherness. This raises the challenging question I posed in that chapter: can somebody be a Christian on their own? Does it make sense?

This points to a further meaning of baptism. Baptism means 'you are beloved' and it also means 'you are welcomed'. To be baptised means to belong. It is not about having something 'done' to a person. It is to join, to become a member, to become part of the community of those who gather to celebrate the Eucharist together. It is a call to participate, to travel together in a shared joy and hope

Unfortunately this is obscured by the way baptism is usually conducted. It is usually just family and friends. It is apart from the gathering of the Christian community. This gives the misleading impression that a person's baptism is their own affair only. It carries little sense of anything happening in the community and to the community. I will take up this theme of community again in a later chapter.

(It is also obscured by the practice of baptising people as infants. To correct this, the emphasis in infant baptism is now on welcoming the baby into the Christian family. The hope is that, as the child grow up, they will make this sense of belonging their own.)

*Holiness*

Third, being a Christian is a call to holiness. But 'holy' is a problematic word. It seems to be taking us out of the ordinary, into a more rarefied realm, into a world more like that of priests and religious. Sometimes it can also have a hint of something self-righteous and presumptuous. But in fact holiness is quite ordinary.

In the New Testament Christians are referred to as saints, which is the same word as holy. For instance, the letters to the Philippians, the Ephesians and the Colossians are addressed to 'the saints' in those places. Paul begins his letters to the Romans and to the Corinthians by addressing them as 'called to be saints'. Here, saints are not people who are being rewarded in another life, but people who are having a certain kind of experience in this one.

Christians are saints, they are holy; meaning that they are blessed. They experience themselves as having been blessed with hearing the good news of the gospel. They feel themselves blessed for having been called and gathered into the assembly of thanksgiving that is the Eucharist.

This is what holiness is about. Being holy is, first and foremost, about something God does. It is what we are by virtue of God's gracing us as God's beloved. Only then is it something we do. It is our call to live up to this reality, to enter into this dignity. It is the call to 'become what you are'.

The holy person is somebody who is making their call a real experience in the present. It is not somebody who withdraws from ordinary life, but somebody who seeks to integrate their faith into their life and their life into their faith. Holiness is about entering into the challenge of the calling, with all the self-purification and discipline and renunciation which that entails.

We are hampered from seeing it this way because of the 'two-tier' spirituality of the past. I am thinking, for instance, of how it used to be said that the religious life is a higher vocation than that of marriage; because it is free of the distractions of ordinary life. In contrast to this, the contemporary experience of spirituality should help us to appreciate holiness. Spirituality today is about living ordinary life at depth, going beyond the surface to access the 'more' in the everyday.

Somebody asked the question: of all the thousands of saints canonised in the 2000 years of Christianity, how many were mothers or fathers? The question shows up how institutionalised is the identification of holiness with clergy and religious. We know, in fact, that the vast majority of saints will never be canonised. They are unnamed, uncelebrated. Their problem is that they are too ordinary. Holiness, saintly living, in the real meaning of the terms, is exceedingly widespread.

*Discernment*

A fourth meaning of vocation is that it is a journey. Our calling is not a single event. It may be rooted in baptism but it happens again and again. John Henry Newman puts it well:

> All through our life Christ is calling us. He called us first in baptism; but afterwards also ... he calls us on from grace to grace, and from holiness to holiness, while life is given us ... but we are slow to master the great truth ... We do not understand that his call is a thing which takes place now. We think it took place in the apostles' days, but we do not believe in it, we do not look out for it in our own case.[31]

Our calling is a journey of discovery and it hinges on the quality of our discernment. The Bible tells the story of Samuel, who hears a call but does not realise that it is coming from the Lord (1 Samuel 3:1-10). Likewise, in our daily lives, God's call comes to us again and again, but we may not recognise that this is what it is.

I am not talking about some strange 'call experience'. Rather, the voice of our experience is the voice of God. The Christian vocation is a journey into our experience of life, which is at the same time a journey into God. We are developing our capacity to see our life's experiences with the eyes of faith, to hear what God is saying to us in the ordinary events of our lives.

We hear this call most concretely in the call of others around us. We hear it from those who encourage us and believe in us, from those who challenge us and bring out the best in us. And we hear it in prayer. We hear it in the kind of prayer that attends to what is going on in our lives and that says, like Samuel: 'Speak, Lord, for your servant is listening.'

*Different forms, same vocation*
So far I have been talking about the vocation common to all Christians. At the same time, vocation is varied, diverse, lived differently by each person. Each one is 'called by name', therefore vocation is individuated by each person. We each put our own stamp on it, the stamp of our own personality, of our unique experience of life, of the life-choices we make, our commitments and occupations.

We have made the mistake of thinking that certain life-choices – religious life and priesthood – are the whole of vocation. But that is simply the specific form it takes for some people. This, though, raises an interesting question. If vocation is about all of us, what is the vocation of the priest or religious?

First the priest. One priest I know spent some years of his ministry in South America. After coming home he was asked the difference between the church here and the church there. His reply was: 'In Ireland the people help the priest; in Peru the priest helps the people.' This says succinctly that the priest's vocation is to help other people in their vocation.

The current Catholic *Catechism* says the same. All Christians have the same vocation to allow the grace and truth of their baptism to unfold in their lives. What is different about the vocation of the priest is that it is 'at the service of ... the unfolding of the baptismal grace of all'.[32] This thought suggests that we should think first, not of the priest, but of ourselves as a baptised community. Then we will see where the priest fits in.

In the case of religious, we tend to think in terms of how different they are. They do not marry or accumulate possessions, their lifestyle is poles apart. But if we thought about what they are instead of what they are not, we would say something different. We might say that they dedicate their lives to doing good for others; that they live in community; and that they find God in all this.

But is that not the same as every Christian? We find ourselves in giving ourselves. We live in community (family for most of us). God becomes real and close in just this. I am saying that the vocation of religious, through their radical style of life, is to mirror to each Christian their own vocation. It is appropriate that they are called 'sisters' and 'brothers'. They are not strange but familiar, companions in the same calling.

In the last chapter I spoke about Christian morality in terms of discipleship. The word belongs here too. Discipleship is a word for the calling of every baptised person as I have been describing it. Discipleship is what vocation is mainly about. The vocation of priest or religious is secondary to the vocation of baptism. It is at the service of the discipleship of all.

### A vocations crisis?

In recent times we have been talking about a 'vocations crisis' in the church. The ideas of this chapter have something important to say about how we understand this so-called crisis. I will suggest three different meanings of the phrase.

The first and obvious one is that there is a shortage of priests and religious. 'Shortage' is a relative term however. It may mean 'less than before', but there may still be a lot more priests and religious than elsewhere in the world. Still, when we see the crisis in this way, we are usually asked to 'pray for vocations' and to 'foster vocations'.

But praying for vocations relates to only a very small percentage of the baptised. In the case of priests, the vocations will not come from women or married people or gay people, because of the restrictions in place. Many people now see that the 'crisis' is actually a crisis in the way that the church defines vocation, so as to exclude the vast majority of it members.

The third meaning may be the most important. It is when large numbers of baptised Christians have no sense of calling. Perhaps they see themselves as recipients of services. Perhaps they have little sense of active engagement. Perhaps they see themselves as outsiders looking in. That may be the greatest vocations crisis; when baptised people have not discovered their own baptism.

### For reflection

How has your own vocation as a Christian evolved over the years? Where does the Christian community come into it?

CHAPTER TWENTY-ONE

## *My Mission in Life*

Vocation is one side of the coin; mission is the other. The Christian is called by name, and then the Christian is sent. 'Mission' means sending and this chapter teases out what it means to be sent; our mission in life as Christians.

Most people would associate the word with the 'foreign missions': missionaries going from Christian lands to proclaim the gospel where it has not been heard. Apart from that, much use of the word today is secular. Most organisations now have a 'mission statement', a focused declaration of who they are and what they are about. And of course there is the adventurous sense of mission, the daring task, the 'mission impossible'.

If, in the church, mission means no more than foreign missions, then mission is something that somebody else is doing. It is an activity that most Christians are not engaged in. Not only that but many would resist being associated with the word. They would not care to think of themselves as 'missionaries'. They would probably be more likely to talk of their Christian calling than of their Christian mission.

In this part of the world, the 'rank-and-file' church members have tended to be on the receiving end. They avail themselves of the services provided for them by the people who are in ministry. There is a weak sense of having an outgoing role, of being a driving force. Maybe it is a lack of self-confidence. Maybe they were never asked. Many seem content to just get on with their lives and keep their religion to themselves.

The following thought of Pope Paul VI captures the challenge. He says that 'It is unthinkable that a person should accept the Word without becoming a person who bears witness to it and proclaims it in their turn.'[33] It is 'unthinkable', he says, that we could separate being called from being sent, that we could receive and not give. And yet we do.

*Receiving and giving*
When we go back to the gospels with this thought in mind, we find that calling and mission are intimately connected. I am

going to look at a number of instances where a person encountered Jesus. In each case the encounter has a shape. It is both a calling and a sending, a receiving and a giving.

Mark's gospel tells the story of a man possessed of an unclean spirit. When he has been healed by Jesus, he begs to stay with him. But Jesus refuses and tells him: 'Go home to your friends and tell them how much the Lord has done for you and what mercy he has shown you' (5:19). Receiving leads to giving but the man, it seems, would have preferred to go on receiving!

John's gospel recounts an encounter with Jesus where a Samaritan woman comes to new levels of self-knowledge and faith. 'Come and see a man who told me everything I have ever done! He cannot be the Messiah, can he?' (4:29). Following from this, many others come to him because of her testimony. What she took in to herself she gives out again for others.

An incident in Luke's gospel captures the 'logic' of it. As Jesus dines with a Pharisee, a woman 'who was a sinner' enters, then bathes his feet, kissing and anointing them. In defence of her to his host Jesus says: 'Her sins, which were many, have been forgiven; hence she has shown great love' (7:47). Her great love is the giving. It is the outflow from what she has received, from her forgiven heart.

Again in Luke (chapter 19), Jesus visits the house of Zacchaeus, a rich and despised tax-collector. The visit is an experience of forgiveness and conversion. Zacchaeus commits to giving half his possessions to the poor and to more than compensating anyone he has defrauded. The generosity of his giving matches the amount that he has received. What he received became an impulse to give.

Finally, Jesus articulates this pattern himself when he washes the feet of his companions at his final meal with them. 'If I, your Lord and Teacher, have washed your feet, you also ought to wash one another's feet' (John 13:14). The one ministered to is to minister in turn. The pattern is: first called, then sent.

Reflecting on these encounters, note who it is that is called. It is often the most unlikely person. It is not the best, but the broken. It is the woman; it is the one out in the cold; it is the outsider; it is the one who is despised. When Jesus calls a person by name, boundaries are broken, expectations are surprised.

What happens when he calls is related to who the person is and to their circumstances. For one person it is an experience of being accepted. For another, it is healing. For another, their own self is revealed to them. For another, forgiveness is received. For another, it is about being challenged to a larger vision. In each case the call is specific. It comes to a person where they are at. The call touches on their tears and hope.

This, then, moves into a giving. The Samaritan woman left her water jar (John 4:28), just as other disciples left their fishing nets. It is a move into a new reality, a new phase in the person's life story. The one who is gifted learns to see themselves as gift. In Henri Nouwen's celebrated phrase, mission is about becoming 'the wounded healer'. The one so in need of grace is now the channel of grace.

What is received into the heart is focused outwards. What the Christian receives in being called is not for hoarding. And what is received is not diminished by giving. Quite the contrary: reaching out is what makes it real, what gives it depth. In assenting to being sent I discover what it is to be called. And if there is no sending, no sense of mission, the call has been only superficially explored. Only a fraction has been received.

*Mission and community*
The mission of each individual Christian follows this same gospel pattern. Each person is called, just as they are, in the particular circumstances of their life. And the calling becomes a sending, just as it did for the people who encountered Jesus in the gospels. We now need to add to this picture the element of community.

In the chapter on church, I said that the original meaning of mission was God's mission, God's reaching out to humanity in Christ. This gives birth to a community of disciples centred on continuing God's mission. Church is this mission-centred community. And the mission of each individual Christian has its meaning within that context.

The mission of each Christian is not an individual adventure, a kind of 'lone ranger' assignment. It begins with a movement into community. It is a mission to belong, to enter into the community called church and to be formed in its identity. This is where we can situate the meaning of the sacrament of confirmation.

We see baptism as the sacrament of our calling or vocation, and confirmation as the sacrament of our sending or mission. But it is significant for our discussion that, originally, baptism and confirmation were not two sacraments, but parts of a single ritual of initiation of adults into the community.

Confirmation was originally the concluding part of the baptism rite. Here the candidates were blessed by the bishop with the oil of chrism and dismissed (again that word 'sent'). But where were they sent? They were not sent into the world, but into the Eucharist. This was the final stage of initiation, where they participated fully in the Eucharist for the first time. So 'confirmation' means firstly this sending into the community.

Joining in the Eucharistic assembly leads into the second stage of the individual's mission. For the Eucharist itself concludes with a dismissal, a sending. (We noted earlier that the word 'Mass' derives from the word mission.) Those who have gathered, the community of disciples, are sent into the world, in the power of the Spirit, to continue God's mission among humanity.

It is easy to miss how central this is to the Eucharist. In the past we were conditioned to think of Mass as a duty. We thought that when the Mass was over the duty was done. But Mass is only 'done' when it is lived. It is only fully celebrated when it flows into mission. Thus the person who is called is sent, first into the community and then, with the community, into the world.

If we think that 'going to Mass' is the be-all and end-all of being a Christian, this gets pushed into the background. We fail to recognise that mission is the whole *raison d'être* of church, the very reason for Christianity. Maybe it is Eucharist that should be in the background? And yet, at the same time, the original meaning of the word church is the gathering of Christians for the breaking of bread.

It is not either-or but both-and. Both Eucharist and mission are the centre of Christianity. The Christian is sent in this twofold sense, both into the community and into the world. Thus Vatican II called the Eucharist the 'source' and the 'summit' of Christian action.[34] It is the source that inspires and resources Christians for their mission in the world. And it is the summit to which they bring their labours and exertions.

*Ordinary*

The Christian's mission in the world is not about some special 'religious' kind of activity. It is not about 'evangelising' others in the sense of preaching and converting. It is something more ordinary than that. It is more in the spirit of the words attributed to Francis of Assisi: 'Every Christian is called to preach the gospel, and if necessary to use words.'

Mission is not mainly about words. It is about the quality of a person's presence among others. It is precisely in this that we continue God's mission in Jesus. Jesus' life hinged on his compassion and solidarity. It is the same for his disciples. Mission is about living lives of compassion and solidarity, inspired by his spirit. It is about hope-filled living, radiating to others the good news of the gospel (which is what the related word 'evangelisation' means).

Neither is mission about special people set apart. We tend to think about people with special attributes, who are specially chosen. But it is quite the opposite, as the gospel stories above show. Those who are sent are surprisingly ordinary. They themselves might have been the last to suspect that they have so much to give.

To illustrate this, we could think of a time when we ourselves have been graced by unexpected people. Maybe it was somebody who was sick; or a child; or somebody else who seemingly had nothing to offer. We are graced unexpectedly, by those least expected to be missionaries. This echoes the words of Paul: 'Consider your own call; not many of you were wise by human standards, not many were powerful, not many were of noble birth' (1 Corinthians 1:26).

And mission is not about special places. We might be inclined to see it as taking place in 'churchy' contexts. But the mission we are talking about happens in the ordinary situations of people's daily lives. It happens in our families, in our relationships, in our neighbourhood and community, at our work and leisure. Mission is about who we are where we are, and the presence we can be just there. It is about the real world we live in and how Christianity can inspire us to make that world a better place.

*Images for mission*

I want to conclude with three images for the mission of the Christian. One image is that of sun and moon. The moon has no light of its own. When we look at the moon, it is the reflected light of the sun that we see. In a similar way, when the Christian reaches out in mission, it is Christ that people experience.

The second comes from the novel *The Secret Scripture*. There is a character in the story, a priest, who is not in touch at all with his calling. In a compelling image, he is depicted thus: 'He was like a singer who knows the words and can sing, but cannot sing the song as conceived in the heart of the composer. Mostly he was dry.'[35]

In mission, the composer is Jesus and the song is his life. Mission happens when we are captivated by Jesus' vision, by the energy of his passion, by the imagination that inspired his song. We receive that captivation as a gift, a grace. But it impels us out again, to sing the song ourselves. That is precisely the kind of gift or captivation it is. Our Christian mission is nothing other than our lives becoming that song, filled with his passion and his spirit.

A third image is that of carrying Jesus. Rowan Williams, the Archbishop of Canterbury, offered this interpretation of the story of Mary visiting Elizabeth (Luke 1:39):

> Mary appears to us here as the first missionary, the first human being to bring the good news of Jesus Christ to another; and she does it simply by carrying Christ within her. She reminds us that mission begins not in delivering a message in words but in the journey towards another person with Jesus in your heart. She testifies to the primary importance of simply carrying Jesus, even before there are words or deeds to show him and explain him.[36]

Mission is about who we are and the quality of our presence. When Jesus is real for us, and when we think in terms of other people, we are carrying Jesus. The light and hope of Christ radiate from us.

These images could suggest that the individual is no more than a conduit. But it is not so. While it is the spirit of Jesus in us, it is our personality, our individuality. It is the particular and distinctive person that each one of us is that reflects the light, that sings the song, that carries Jesus. Our mission carries the stamp of who we are.

There is also something here that is bigger than Christianity. Just as everybody is called, by virtue of being a human person, so too everybody is sent. As Christians we do not stand above but beside many others who are reaching out to be a life-giving presence in the world.

Outside Christianity there are many others who are living value-centred, other-centred lives. When we are in touch with our mission as Christians, that should also open our eyes to these others. They too are continuing God's mission simply by the quality of their human lives.

*For reflection*
Think of times when you were the recipient, when somebody came to you with the good news of the gospel, when you were 'evangelised'. What do those times tell you about mission?

CHAPTER TWENTY-TWO

# *Believing is Belonging*

Being called and being sent go together. But they happen in the context of a community of Christians. I now want to focus more on community, which was a theme in both the previous chapters as well as in the chapter about church. I will spell out more of what it means to live Christianity in a together way.

## *The provided-for church*

How do we transcend privacy and see our Christianity in a more 'corporate' way? Part of it is appreciating where we have come from and how this affects the way we see ourselves as members of church. I am thinking here of the link between clericalism and privacy, how a clerical culture has made for a privatised spirituality.

The earliest Christians, I have said, were less a church than a spirit-inspired movement. We can see this in Paul's letters. He lists different ways in which the Spirit 'graces' or 'energises' people. In his lists he mentions gifts of compassion, healing, prophecy, cheerfulnesss, teaching (1 Corinthians 12; Romans 12; Ephesians 4). By way of summary he says: 'To each is given the manifestation of the Spirit for the common good' (1 Corinthians 12:7).

This is where the word 'ministry' comes from. It did not originally refer to an ecclesiastical position, but had to do with all the people. In different ways people 'ministered' to one another. In their diverse energies or giftedness they were of service to one another. Thereby they were building up the community, which Paul calls the 'body' of Christ.

Think of the way the word is used at the end of Jesus' time in the desert: 'angels came and ministered to him' (Mark 1:13). This is not churchy language, it is quite homely. It captures the spirit of how Christians were with one another and for one another in those early days. It was 'church' in a highly participative mode.

As history unfolded, church came to be identified with hierarchy. The variety and richness of ministries was swallowed up into the ministry of the clergy. Ministry was now what the clergy did for the laity. Even the word 'laity' implies as much. It is suggestive of an outsider looking in. It is to be on the receiving end, passive, submissive. This is reflected in how the people were to become more like spectators in the old Mass.

(Clericalism, though, is not confined to church, even if the word is. Other walks of life have their 'clergy', for instance the medical or the legal profession. They are the insiders, the experts, with the attendant status. The rest of us are 'lay', that is, on the outside, unqualified, incompetent, deferential. Here, as in the church, 'lay' defines people by what they are not.)

Thus we ended up with what has been called a 'provided for' church. In Ireland it peaked around the 1950s, with huge numbers of priests and religious. While they provided an extraordinary service – parishes, schools, hospitals – there was a downside. The laity were 'spoiled', as it were, rendered more passive, set more firmly into a provided-for mindset.

Parishes today complain of how hard it is to get people involved. A significant part of the difficulty is that people have been conditioned into the opposite. Over generations they have become used to being provided for, to having everything done for them. That does not change overnight. The provided-for parish has a journey to travel before it becomes a 'self-ministering' community

All this feeds into the privatising of Christianity. As people are alienated from the ownership of their own Christian community, faith tends to become a private practice and devotion. This is so even at a public ceremony such as the Mass. Church is less a community of disciples and more a collection of individuals serviced by an institution.

Also today, many who do not participate in church (but who were baptised) see the church as a service-provider. When a child is born they return for baptism. When a parent dies they return for the funeral liturgy. It is as if being baptised is a kind of membership card, giving entitlement to various services, however rarely they are availed of. There is little in the way of belonging.

The sociologist Grace Davie has styled this 'vicarious religion'.[37] It is when religion is practised by a minority 'on behalf' as it were of a much larger number. We might wonder, though, how long this will continue. Without an active sense of belonging, will it gradually fade away?

*A ministering community*

We are left, then, with weak levels of belonging. We have the person who only comes to church when in need of one of its services. There is the person who comes, but takes part in a quite private capacity or for some purely personal benefit. There is the person who comes only to receive, not seeing any more active form of engagement as part of their Christian identity.

Real belonging goes further than any of this. It is to have a strong sense that we are members of a people's church, not a clerical church. Church is not a flock ministered to by priests. It is not a community ministered to, in the absence of priests, by pastoral councils and pastoral workers. Church is a ministering community. That is how it originally was. The role of clergy and other leaders is to facilitate this, not to replace it.

In the church we are meant to belong in this strong sense. It is not like having a library card, seldom borrowing a book yet remaining fully a member. And belonging to the Christian community, it seems to me, is a combination of two things. On the one hand, we identify with the core message. On the other, we identify with a specific faith community.

The core message is the good news of the gospel. To identify with it is to believe in Jesus Christ and all that he means. Believing is far more than accepting the teachings of the church. It is not primarily about doctrines but about a person. But this believing is not separate from belonging. It is not to be made into a private experience.

So believing is also belonging. And belonging is local. It is not simply that believers belong to the universal church. That could be more anonymous than the library. It is meant to be like how things were at the start, where 'church' meant the people who gathered in this particular place. Originally, to believe meant to belong in this very definite way.

Belonging in that local way means we feel part of a particular community. It means we feel welcome and accepted. It means we feel connected to others. It means we feel accompanied and

supported. It means we participate. It means we bring our distinctive contributions to the table. It means we have a 'corporate
identity' as Christians.

*Belonging in action*
Let us describe what this belonging might look like practically.
First, there is our daily ministering as members of a ministering
community. As Jesus washed Peter's feet, we follow his call to
do as he did. This includes allowing ourselves be ministered to,
as Peter had to learn. We live what we believe, in all our relationships and wherever we go. The quality of our ministering
makes our relationships into relationships of grace.

Some people think that life is one thing and religion another.
They think that religion is just what goes on in churches. They
may not have appreciated that the most spiritual thing of all is
daily life. We might not use the word 'ministering' for it, yet it
deserves to be honoured for what it is. Ministering happens
when our living and our relating are expressive of our faith and
hope and love.

In our daily ministering, we have a sense of 'the body', the
corporate sense of being members of the body of Christ, the
community of disciples. We have the feeling that our believing
connects us to others who are walking the same path, engaged
in the same mission. We feel that we are each a piece of the jigsaw, that our efforts are not isolated, that they add up to something bigger, a bigger pattern.

Next, we gather to participate in the community's celebration of the Eucharist. Our daily ministering feeds into this and
issues out of it. Our sense of being part of 'the body' is intensified when we gather and meet and encounter each other in this
setting. Obviously, I am talking here of a regular, frequent participation in the Eucharist.

But I am not talking about the old sense of 'going to Mass', as
if this were the only duty incumbent upon us. The gospel accounts of the Last Supper tell us of the breaking of bread and of
the washing of feet. Christian living is both. It is Eucharist and it
is daily living. In the Eucharist Christ ministers to us and then
we minister to one another. Our liturgy and our life are intimately one. They make little sense apart from each other.

For all this to be as I describe, certain things have to happen. We have to feel that we are together. The Eucharist has to be a social experience, an experience of togetherness. And we have to be able to bring our lives to the altar. We do not leave them in the porch, as if irrelevant to what goes on inside the church. But we bring our whole selves to the table of the Lord.

### The body

I know of no more eloquent expression of this than that of Augustine in a sermon to newly baptised (adult) Christians, around the year 400. This was at the final moment of their initiation, when they were admitted to full participation in the Eucharist. He is explaining to them, in the manner of revealing a secret, the meaning of what is about to unfold – how the bread is the body of Christ and the chalice his blood.

He explains by quoting the words of Paul: 'You are the body of Christ and his members' (1 Corinthians 12:27). The emphasis is on 'You'. And from this he concludes: 'It is your own mystery that has been placed on the table of the Lord. It is your own mystery that you receive.'[38] This is hardly what people today would expect to hear. We are being confronted with ancient yet very novel perspectives.

Augustine unpacks what he means with the imagery of how bread and wine are made. In the making of wine, the juice of many grapes flows into one. That, he says, is how Christ wants us to belong to him, to pour into him as it were. He concludes: 'It is the mystery of our peace and unity which he consecrates on his table.'

He draws on the imagery of making bread to speak of the steps in the Christian's initiation into the body. The grains being ground down corresponds to being exorcised. The bread's being moistened corresponds to baptism. Its being baked corresponds to the fire of the Spirit (our confirmation). And he concludes: 'Be what you see and accept what you are.'

It is we ourselves who have been placed on the table of the Lord. It is we who are consecrated, we who are changed and transformed into the body of Christ. So, says Augustine, when the minister says 'Body of Christ' and we respond 'Amen', we are saying Amen (yes, so be it) to what we are. Eucharist concludes with our being sent to become what we are. 'So be a member of Christ's body, that your Amen may be true'.

We are used to thinking of Mass as the consecration, bread and wine changed into the body and blood of Christ. Augustine is thinking of communion, of our being changed into the body of Christ. We think of communion as receiving the body of Christ into our souls. Augustine sees it almost the other way around. As I quoted in the chapter on Eucharist, he speaks of our 'being digested into his body and being turned into his members, so that we may be what we receive'.

The two go together, but we lost sight of the second. We reduced the body of Christ to something that we receive and forgot that it is what we become. In the process we reduced our corporate identity to an individual identity. 'Corporate', I should say, derives from the Latin *corpus* for body, as in *Corpus Christi*. As Christians, we are so much more than individuals. We are a corporate person in whom many individuals participate.

Eucharist (like every sacrament) is primarily something that happens to the community, to those gathered, rather than to the individuals present. In our tradition of privacy we have imagined that individuals go to Mass and receive grace. The truth is that we gather and that we celebrate our transformation into the body of Christ. That is how we belong. And this is what brings to our daily ministering the strong sense of being members of the body, pieces of the jigsaw.

*The parish*

I am offering a picture of what belonging looks like – daily ministering, our sense of the body, our participation in Eucharist, celebrating who we are, our return to daily ministering with a heightened sense of the body. Next, that daily ministering may also include more specific involvements in the Christian community.

Many people shy away from 'getting involved'. But what matters most is feeling involved – in the way just described. The heart of being involved is daily ministering and participating in the Eucharist, with a strong sense of belonging to the body. At the same time, some of the community take on more specific tasks.

These are often called 'ministries'. Within the liturgy we have ministers of the Eucharist and of the Word, we have choirs and liturgy teams. Outside of the Eucharist parishes have many ministry groups engaged a variety of activities: leadership, caring, outreach, spirituality, administration.

Two reservations might be expressed here. If being involved is too identified with these ministries, it takes away from seeing the ordinary daily ministering of everybody as the basic meaning of ministry. The issue in most parishes is not getting people involved. It is affirming people, so that they can see how they are already involved.

The other reservation is about giving the impression that being involved has to be parish-based. As it is, many Christians practise their faith on other fronts. For instance, many parents are involved in local sports clubs. Many adults work with the poor or homeless or elderly, or in other forms of social care. Because it is not parish-based it may not be noticed by the parish. But it is equally deserving of being brought to the altar.

A final thought about 'parish'. Parish is meant to be a Eucharistic community, a family of people who gather to celebrate the Eucharist. In many parts of the world there is little access to Eucharist, because there are so few priests. But there is a very strong sense of Christian community. In our part of the world it can be the reverse. There is easy access to Eucharist, but there is a weaker sense of being a community of disciples, the body of Christ.

Unfortunately this is reflected in what the word parish often means. It suggests a geographical territory, an administrative unit of the church. It suggests buildings, the church, the presbytery, the school, the hall. It suggests services, from baptisms and funerals to Mass cards and getting forms signed. Many would never think of it as being primarily about people and community. The word needs to be redeemed.

We are moving today from seeing parish as a structure and towards seeing it as an experience; as sharing and offering a particular kind of experience. It is not just an experience of uplifting Masses and music, because that can remain private and anonymous. It is an experience of belonging, of welcome, of feeling involved and cared for. It is an experience of connection, of participation, of mission. It is an experience of being a piece of the jigsaw, a member of the body.

*For reflection*
Identify one practical step you could take, to move yourself away from practising Christianity in a private capacity and towards practising it in a together way.

CHAPTER TWENTY-THREE

# *Prayer*

In 'living the life' prayer is key. It is meant to be at the heart of everyday Christian life. And because we live our Christianity as members of the community of disciples, prayer is both an individual and a community practice. The focus here is on what this prayer is, and what it actually looks like.

## *The reality*
The reality varies a lot. For some people, prayer is a very important part of their lives. There are others, who also live a committed Christian life, who seem to get by with very little by way of prayer. But, where there is prayer in the everyday life of Christians, its quality varies a lot.

From years ago I recall my mother saying to me that one of her favourite prayers was from the psalm: 'Be still and know that I am God' (Psalm 46:10). It was a moment of revelation into the inner life of somebody I had lived with all my life. It has led me to appreciate that there are many contemplatives hidden among us, people who are seriously prayerful, living their Christian lives with real intensity

But the reality often falls short of that. In many cases, prayer means 'saying prayers'. It is little more than the mechanical repetition of words and formulas. Also, such prayer can have little or no relation of life. I can be saying the Our Father, 'As we forgive those who trespass against us', without adverting at all to the bitterness I have felt towards somebody for the last week.

Then there is prayer that has no communal aspect to it, purely private, between 'me and God'. Even Mass, as I have said, may be no more than a private devotion. That is not to say that the prayer is not real. It may even be yearning for something more than the private. But it is not yet what Christian prayer is meant to be, a together thing, personal but not exclusively private.

At the same time, communal prayer itself sometimes hardly deserves the name of prayer. It can be little more than routine formulas being recited mindlessly: 'words, words, words', with little depth of engagement. Sad to say, Sunday Eucharist can fail to be prayerful. It can fail to be an experience of prayer.

Then there are people in whose lives there is effectively no prayer at all. The unreflected life, as Plato called it, is all around us. Many, maybe most of us, are unable to stop, to make space, to stand back. We are imprisoned in our own busyness, we are 'time-poor'. Perhaps we are afraid of the stillness and what might surface from within when we make space to be still.

Meanwhile, many people are finding nourishment in other places than Christianity. There are different forms of spiritual exercises that people are finding very valuable in focusing and centring their lives. In ways other than what is traditionally known as prayer, people are connecting with themselves and with something greater than themselves.

*The still point*
Christian prayer is more than saying prayers. But it is also more than what today we call meditation, valuable and all as that meditating is. Christian prayer is about an Other (and also about others, as we will see). It is not a solitary exercise, it is not alone time. It is an encounter, interpersonal, interactive.

I spoke already of Christianity's strong sense of the intersection of time and timelessness, centred on the incarnation. We human beings live in time; as in T.S. Eliot's poem, 'Time before and time after', 'Time past and time future'.[39] We live in a flow of happening, with joys and worries, with concerns that preoccupy us only to give way to new concerns.

In contrast to this stream of time, God is timeless, more like an eternal now, to whom all this time is present at once. One of the psalms pictures it well:

> The Lord looks down from heaven; he sees all humankind.
> From where he sits enthroned he watches
> all the inhabitants of the earth,
> he who fashions the hearts of them all
> and observes all their deeds (Psalm 33:13-15).

Prayer is about being at the point of intersection where God is, at what Eliot calls 'the still point of the turning world'.

Yet, at this point, God can appear to be a cold and remote entity. There may be no sense of closeness and ease. There may be more anxiety than intimacy. We find ourselves praying with apprehension, in hope of a favourable response. We are praying as if the response cannot be relied upon, as if there is no commitment from beyond. God is aloof, a stranger, not to be presumed upon.

But Incarnation means that God inhabits this point of intersection. 'The Word became flesh and lived among us' (John 1:14) translates literally as 'pitched his tent'. God has made this point of intersection God's abode. This God is intimate, near, warm. The Lord indeed 'looks down from heaven' but has also come close with infinite compassion.

So prayer is not engaging with God in some undefined and impersonal way. It is engaging with the God of Jesus Christ; a God who has a face, whose 'self-portrait' is Jesus. Therefore Christian prayer is always Christ-prayer. It is set within the relationship of discipleship.

We might pause here a moment to consider Jesus' own prayer. The gospels depict him as frequently going off alone to pray (eg Mark 1:35). They show him praying at important or difficult moments in his life, such as his own baptism (Luke 3:21), the murder of John the Baptist (Matthew 14:13), his message being rejected (Matthew 11:25), before choosing the twelve (Luke 6:12), after the feeding of the thousands (Matthew 14:23), on the night before he died (Luke 22:41; John 17), as well as on the cross (eg Mark 15:34).

Prayer is at the centre. But there is also a sense of his life being 'double-centred'. It is centred on his God. And it is centred on what this God is centred on, which is fullness of life for God's people. His life is an interaction or interplay between these two centres; the prayer that is centred on God and the living that is centred on what God is centred on.

The prayer of Christians takes its shape from this. It is the place where we go to attend to him and our relationship with him, in the same kind of way as a wife and husband would give 'quality time' to being together. The relationship itself is enriched and avowed at a deeper level because of this. And our living becomes expressive of the relationship in ever fuller ways, becomes more 'Christian'.

What is happening is that our Christian self is being

constructed out of the interaction. We bring a different self to our living. Our living is more and more reflective of our discipleship, as our Christian self is being constructed more and more. That in turn feeds back into more profound prayer time. It is an ongoing spiral, where prayer has become the 'engine' of discipleship.

## The variety of prayer

Here I want to sketch out different forms that prayer can take. This will show the variety of what is possible. And it will take us beyond the association of prayer with merely saying prayers and with asking God for something.

First, prayer is both an individual and a communal practice. I have been stressing that discipleship is a communal calling and this applies to prayer also. If it is seen as just individual, then prayer will be no more than a private affair. Even the Eucharist, the pre-eminent communal prayer, will be reduced to a private spiritual exercise.

But if discipleship is a communal thing, praying together becomes highly significant. Not only is prayer an interaction with the Other, the God of Jesus Christ. It is also an interaction with others. Those others are our fellow members of the body of Christ, both this local Christian community and beyond. Prayer is, as it were, vertical and horizontal. It links us in a community of being both with the divine source of our being and with our companions in discipleship.

The prayer that is the Eucharist is communal in a special sense. We are praying with others to the Other, but it is more than that. When we are with our fellow disciples we are more than a collection of disciples. As the last chapter presented it, we are the body of Christ, the corporate person in whom there are many individual disciples. It is not just each of us in our separate relationships with the Lord. It is all of us together in a single, shared relationship with him.

Praying with one another has very practical benefits. It overcomes isolation. It strengthens the sense of a shared identity, a shared vocation, a shared mission. It brings the balance of shared perspectives. It opens us to being inspired by others. It encourages us in living as disciples, with a feeling of being 'in it together'. It also brings a sense that we accompanied by these others when we are praying on our own.

It might be assumed that individual prayer is more personal than communal prayer. But in fact praying together can be just as profound a spiritual experience. Coming together to pray, we experience the truth of Jesus' words: 'Where two or three are gathered in my name, I am there among them' (Matthew 18:20). When we pray together it can be easier to feel his presence than when we pray alone. It certainly assures us of his presence.

Whether together or on our own, prayer has a variety of modes or moods. The following paragraphs briefly describe these; the prayers of thanks, of adoration, of contrition, of silence, of lament and of petition. If we go to the Bible, we can find the whole variety of different moods among its 150 psalms.

*Thanks*

Our prayer can be in the forms of thanks. In our family we have prayer time before bed with the children. As it happens, most of the prayers are saying thanks for things that have happened during the day. Perhaps this is the most natural form of prayer; or at least it can become the most natural. We can grow into a constant outlook of gratitude for the grace that is always offering itself to us in life. We can find ourselves enjoying the gift of life more and more.

Thanks is not given just for the good things that come our way. That would leave many with little to give thanks for. It is more that Christians know God to be present and constant throughout all that we experience, from fortune to misfortune. Indeed, in giving thanks we find that 'fortune' and 'misfortune' are not always what they seem to be at first. A thankful heart is like a self-fulfilling prophecy; it is always discovering cause for thanks.

Eucharist means thanksgiving and it is a together prayer of thanks. At its heart is the thanks Jesus gave, not when good things came his way, but on the night before he died. We gather to give thanks in the Spirit that he did. We are challenged, amidst our joys and troubles, to rediscover the cause for thanks at the core of our faith. We are challenged to make our prayer of thanks into a life of thanks.

*Adoration*

Somewhat similar to thanks is the prayer of adoration and praise. But there is a difference. In thanksgiving, we are usually thanking God for something, be it the blessings of the day or comfort in troubles or whatever. But our adoration and praise is not for anything. It is simply because God is God.

Adoration is the stance that befits us as creatures before our Creator. We do speak of adoring in other contexts; lovers adore each other, people adore certain foods or clothes or music. But only God can truly be adored. In adoration we are tuning in to the most basic relationship we know.

*Contrition*

Contrition, or sorrow, is another mood in which we pray. Besides our goodness and the wonder of our being, there is our fragility and fallibility and the sin in which we all stand. The prayer of contrition acknowledges this. It is characterised by openheartedness. We open ourselves to God, honestly and humbly. Or at least we try to; perhaps we are never capable of being fully openhearted.

But more than that, the prayer of contrition allows God to be God, the God of infinite compassion, the God who is our justific-ation. It allows us hear Jesus say: 'You are future'. Rather than define ourselves by our guilty past, we can live from the future that he sees for us. In allowing ourselves to be forgiven, we open ourselves to transformation.

There is a communal form of this prayer too, the communal sacrament of reconciliation (see chapter 26 below), though it is underused and undervalued. Its focus is celebrating the God of forgiveness. It helps us achieve what can be very hard when praying alone. Its fellowship of prayer helps us into that space where we can believe we are forgiven and rejoice that we are future.

*Silence*

The very opposite of 'saying prayers' is the prayer that has no words, the prayer of silence and contemplation. Somebody compared it to sunbathing. In sunbathing we stop doing any-thing. We just get ourselves into a place where the sun can get at us. But the prayer of silence is more than relaxing. Relaxing is part of it, but it is with a view to concentrating, an intensified concentration that focuses on God. It is the deepest communication that has no words, a mutual presence.

It might sound very solitary, but it can also be a together prayer. In fact, when people gather together for silent prayer, or adoration, it can be easier to enter into the silence than when alone. There is the mood, the setting, a focusing reflection perhaps. All these help in letting go of that 'very energy of thought which keeps thee from thy God'.[40] Often our experience of Eucharist is impoverished by the lack of this prayer of silence.

## Lament

Of the 150 psalms, some are psalms of thanks (e.g. Psalm 107), others are praise (e.g. Psalm 104), others contrition (e.g. Psalm 51). But the biggest category is psalms of lamentation, both individual and communal lament (e.g. Psalms 13, 74). The cry of lamentation to God is perhaps the most recurrent human cry.

In this prayer we may be lamenting our own sufferings or hardship or maltreatment. Or we may lament the pain of others around us, or the pain in the wider world. In that case our lament is also a prayer of consciousness-raising. We are entering into our compassion and we are growing in solidarity. We are entering into the mindset of Jesus.

In the psalms of lamentation, the lament usually moves into a mode of remembering. The people recall the God they believe in. This puts suffering into a healing and hopeful context. It is the same for us. But sometimes the psalm does no more than lament (e.g. Psalm 88). And so again it is with us. Sometimes our prayer is just lament, just darkness, because nothing more is possible at this point.

## Petition

In the prayer of petition we are asking for something, either for ourselves or for others or for the world. While there is an element of this in contrition and in lamentation, we can see now that petition is not the only mode of prayer, not even the main one. But it raises difficult questions; in particular, are our prayers answered, and if so, how? So I will devote the next chapter to discussing it in more detail.

As with the other moods or modes of prayer, lament and

petition are as much communal as individual. Perhaps the most intense form of the prayer of lamentation is when we gather for the funeral of someone we know, especially when the death was tragic. And the most frequent, familiar form of the prayer of petition is when we gather for Eucharist, in the prayers of the faithful.

*Heart space*

Prayer can be as brief as a few seconds. It might be just a 'mindfulness moment'. For that minute all else stops. We step out of the flow of events and become present to ourselves and present to God. It may be a moment of thanks or adoration or contrition or silence or lamentation or petition. For a moment everything is in perspective. The Angelus prayer is an example of a mindfulness moment.

This can lead into a more substantial prayer time each day. Some people find it helpful to have a 'prayer space' in their home. It might be in a corner of a room, perhaps a small table, a candle or an icon or a bible. Ultimately what is going on in all this is the creation of a prayer space within, a prayer space in our heart. That space is the still point, to which we retire frequently, from which we live our Christian lives.

*For reflection*

As you review the different aspects of prayer in this chapter, which are you strong on and which do you think would, if developed, be especially good for you?

CHAPTER TWENTY-FOUR

## *Ask and You Shall Receive*

In this chapter I want to reflect in more detail on the prayer of petition; the prayer where we are asking God for something, be it help or healing, enlightenment, success, love or whatever. Is it the prayer that people say more than any other? My focus is on what it is that is happening in this exchange between ourselves and God.

I will begin with a caricature. Going to bed one evening, a farmer prays to God for rain; the land needs it. In the nearby village a woman prays for sunshine, for tomorrow is her wedding day. What is God supposed to do? After all, Jesus says in the gospels: 'Ask and you will receive' (Matthew 7:7).

Clearly, God does not give everybody what they ask for. It is an impossibility. But then, does God give some people what they ask for, and not others? If some prayers are answered and others not, does that amount to partiality on God's part, favouring some for no apparent reason? Or is it just arbitrary how prayers are answered? Bad people sometimes get what they ask for, while the prayers of good people go unanswered.

A problem with this line of questioning is that it suggests, not just a partial or arbitrary God, but a meddlesome God. We could ask: Does God act in this kind of way at all, intervening and interfering again and again in human affairs? Earlier I suggested that God's relationship to the world might not be along those lines at all. And yet the gospel says: 'Ask and you will receive'.

### What do we want?
Traditionally theology tells us that God does not change. Part of what that means, I think, is that God does not 'chop and change', does not meddle and interfere. Rather, God is constant. God is Spirit, within our human situation, accompanying us. God's Spirit is constant presence, divine energy within us and around us, forever inviting us forth into new freedom.

If this is so, maybe we can let go of thinking that our petitions ask God to make discrete interventions or to bestow specific favours. There is no need of divine intervention because God is already here in the midst of things. Prayer is about connecting with the God already present. It is about accessing what is always available. The issue is not about how God answers. It is about how we ask.

In chapter ten of Mark's gospel, James and John come up to Jesus: 'Teacher, we want you to do for us whatever we ask of you'. He says: 'What do you want me to do for you?' They want to be seated beside him in his glory. 'You do not know what you are asking', he replies. In the next incident, Jesus is walking past a blind beggar, who shouts to him for mercy. Again Jesus asks: 'What do you want me to do for you?' He asks to see again and is healed. He knows what he wants.

The letter of James says: 'You ask and you do not receive, because you ask wrongly, in order to spend what you get on your pleasures' (4:3). He is saying that we can ask wrongly when we ask selfishly. But there are other ways to ask wrongly. We might be asking for what we think we ought to ask for, rather than what we really want. Or we may be asking for what we think we want, when what we really need is something other.

We might differentiate here among our different desires, from our shallow to our deepest desires. Superficial desires may be no more than passing fancies or infatuations or indulgences. Deeper desires relate more to our inner needs, what we need in order to reach new levels of self-realisation as persons. If we live from our shallow rather than our profound desires, we lose touch with ourselves and our own becoming.

This has an important application to prayer. It suggests that, in prayer, we do not need to tell God what we want; God already knows. But do we? Which of our wants are we in touch with? So we need to inform ourselves regarding what we want, and for two reasons. First, in order that we may become more aware, so that our own desires become known to us. Second, so that we grow stronger in our desire.

Prayer of petition is not quite as simple as it looks. It is not a straightforward request-response. It is a learning curve. There is a learning that takes place, out of which the prayer is formed. Going deeper than the superficial, we seek to learn what are our deep desires, which might otherwise remain un-surfaced. And we learn to desire at this depth more intensely.

*A divine conversation*

To understand this learning, I would recall the point from the last chapter, that prayer is interpersonal. We are not alone, just diving deeper into ourselves. We are disciples, who live our lives in relationship with Jesus Christ. The prayer is a conversation; and conversation includes listening as well as talking. This leads me to the following way of visualising the prayer of petition.

The picture I propose is inspired by these two texts from the New Testament. 'It is Christ Jesus who died, yes, who was raised, who is at the right hand of God, who indeed intercedes for us' (Romans 8:34). 'He is able for all time to save those who approach God through him, since he always lives to make intercession for them' (Hebrews 7:25).

It is a powerful picture. Before ever we pray there is a prayer going on, on our behalf, Jesus interceding for us with the Father. Just a few verses earlier, Paul says something very similar, this time speaking of the Spirit. 'The Spirit helps us in our weakness; for we do not know how to pray as we ought, but that very Spirit intercedes with sighs too deep for words' (Romans 8:26).

And he visualises the Spirit as praying within us. 'God has sent the Spirit of his Son into our hearts, crying, Abba! Father!' (Galatians 4:6). Jesus himself prayed: 'Abba! Father' during his life (Mark 14:36). So now he is praying this prayer in us, through the Spirit. Our prayer, which we think we make, is in fact a prayer being carried out within God, Father, Son and Spirit. It is God who prays.

This leads to the idea that, in our prayer of petition, we are entering into the space of that divine prayer. We are at that point of intersection between time and timelessness we spoke about in the last chapter. And we are 'listening in', as it were, to find out what we might hear in that divine conversation. What is Jesus asking for me? What is the Spirit's prayer in me? I listen so as to become part of that prayer, to join my prayer to it.

*Seek ye first*

Maybe this is what Jesus meant when he said: 'I will do whatever you ask in my name' (John 14:13). We do not just pray. We pray in his name. This means that we let our prayer be taken up into his prayer. It is the same idea when Jesus says: 'Strive first for the kingdom of God and all these things will be given to you as well' (Matthew 6:33). God's kingdom was Jesus' passion and the soul of his prayer. Praying in his name means allowing God's kingdom to become the soul of our prayer also.

This takes us to the Our Father, Jesus' prayer that he taught to his disciples. It is the basic prayer of petition. Augustine says: 'If we are praying in the right way, we say nothing that has not already a place in the Lord's prayer'; its words 'give us the framework of true desires'.[41] We can think of it as Jesus' prayer of intercession for us, as the Spirit's 'Abba Father' cry within us.

At we pray this prayer, we are being guided into our deepest desires. In this prayer, says Augustine: 'You may not only learn to ask God for whatever you desire, but also learn what you ought to desire.'[42] There is a convergence here between what we most deeply want and what God most passionately wants for us.

This is the only petition that we can be sure about. In this vein Augustine says: 'There are two things we should ask for with calm assurance: in this world a good life, in the world to come eternal life. About everything else we don't know if it will be good for us.'[43] He gives the examples of one person praying for a wife, another praying to get rich. How do they know this is what will be for their good?

So petition is about aligning our prayer with that of Jesus. To do this is the same as aligning it with our deepest desire. And this is also what the Spirit is praying within us 'with sighs too deep for words'. Such is the process whereby our desires are enlightened and educated, formed and intensified.

In this process we will actually end up with more than we want. When Jesus says: 'Ask and you will receive', he concludes on this note: 'If you, then, who are evil, know how to give good gifts to your children, how much more will the heavenly Father give the Holy Spirit to those who ask him' (Luke 11:13). 'How much more'; the prayer of petition is not a whimpering demand. It is an openness to being surprised.

*Thanks*
All this applies also to the prayer of thanks discussed in the last chapter. Just as we tend to pray for what we want, so we tend to

thank God for what we get. But if we do not know what we want, maybe we do not know what we have received either. And if our petition seeks to align itself with Jesus' intercession, should not our thanks align itself with his thanks?

As we said in the last chapter, Jesus' thanks was not simply for the good fortune in his life. His great prayer of thanks, remarkably, was on the night before he died, as he shared the bread and wine with his companions (Luke 22:17,19). At the lowest point; that was when he gave thanks. He did not give thanks because it was a low point. He gave thanks because he could trust in the movement of grace at all points in his life.

So the prayer of thanks is also a learning curve. In it we discover what to be thankful for. Fundamentally we give thanks for God's grace. But in our prayer we open ourselves to appreciating where that grace is to be found in our lives. We open ourselves to being surprised. We learn to begin our prayer with a simple and unconditional thanks. From there we begin to discover what it is we are thankful for.

*Praying for others*

Up to here, I have been thinking of petitions where we have ourselves in mind. Besides these there are our petitions for others and for the world we live in. So what happens when we pray for others? Is it the same dynamic as just described?

The *Catechism* makes the comment: 'Transformation of the praying heart is the first response to our petition.'[44] That is already evident as regards our petition for ourselves. But also when we pray for others, the one thing that does happen is that we change. At least that should happen. But there is a problem with a lot of petitions, that they are little more than pious aspirations, with no challenge.

For example, we say a prayer for an end to war in the world. But we are letting ourselves off the hook. It would be different were the prayer also a prayer for an increase in our desire for an end to war. It would be different were it a prayer for ourselves as peacemakers, a prayer to become non-violent persons. And it would be different were it also a prayer to increase our solidarity with victims of war and violence, a compassionate praying with them in their situation.

I recall reading about a piece of research into prayer. It discovered that when a person prays for their partner and for the relationship, the prayer makes the person themselves more grateful, more forgiving, more willing to sacrifice. Whatever or whoever we pray for, the first change is in ourselves. If there is not such change, what kind of prayer is it?

But does anybody or anything else change? Take the research quoted. If the prayer changes the one praying, then they are a different presence, and that makes for a changed relationship. But beyond that? Is there any cause-effect when, for instance, we pray for somebody's recovery in illness or for somebody's success in exams? Does our prayer make a difference to them?

This brings us back to the dynamic described above. When we ask God for something for someone else, how do we know that this is what is for their good? How do we know that this is what is most deeply needed? It is just the same as when somebody is praying for their own recovery or their own success. How do they know this is for their good? Here again, we must join our prayer to Jesus' intercession for that person. We must align our prayer to the divine conversation and attune our hearts to God's compassion.

What more can be said? There is a spiritual energy in our world, constantly available. It is the abiding presence of the Spirit of the God of Jesus Christ. Prayer puts us in touch with that presence and passion. We know it can change us when we pray. It can change us when we know we are being prayed for. And even if we do not know we are being prayed for, neither do we comprehend all the workings of that divine energy.

### Prayer and the dead
According to the church, this spiritual energy is also operative between the present life and the next, between ourselves and those whom death has delivered into the sphere of existence beyond time. Paul speaks of the solidarity of the body of Christ; if one person suffers all feel the pain, if one is honoured all share the joy (1 Corinthians 12:26). The idea of 'the communion of saints' is that this solidarity includes those who have died.

The exchange of prayer between ourselves and the dead is seen by the church as an interplay where the prayers and holiness of one can benefit the other. This applies particularly to Purgatory, the final purification a person may undergo in death. But it is seen to work in the other direction also. Besides the living praying for the dead, the prayers of the saints in heaven can help those still on earth.

All this is quite open to caricature. In Cervantes' novel, Don Quixote speaks of how, should Sancho Panza be dead and in purgatory: 'our Holy Mother the Roman Catholic Church can perform ceremonies sufficient to remove you from where you now languish.'[45] Not alone have we let ourselves speak of God meddling on earth. Here we have the church pulling strings in the next world.

In the other direction we are said to benefit from praying to the saints. So, for example, there is the prayer to Saint Anthony to find something that is lost, and to Saint Jude when a situation is hopeless. It is more of the same cause-effect prayer of petition I spoke of. This time we have meddlesome saints alongside a meddlesome God. How do we go beyond such caricature?

Regarding the saints, we might think of them as wholly incorporated into the divine life. Thus they are incorporated also into Jesus' own intercession, rather than operating some independent franchise. When we pray, the witness of an individual saint's life may help us focus. Their particular gift means that they reflect the values of the kingdom in a distinctive way that can inspire us when we pray.

Regarding purgatory, I would recall the idea of prayer happening at that 'still point' of intersection between time and eternity. The question arises: where are these people of purgatory, in time or in eternity? The idea of purgatory as a final purification makes sense, but does it happen in time? If it is beyond time, then our prayer should be formed accordingly. It should be a prayer of waiting in confident hope.

*For reflection*
What do you think of the quotation above from the *Catechism*: 'Transformation of the praying heart is the first response to our petition'?

CHAPTER TWENTY-FIVE

## *Reading the Bible*

This chapter asks: what part does reading the Bible play in a Christian life? I will begin with some general thoughts and then move into specific suggestions of useful ways to read the Bible. Most of the focus is on reading the gospels.

There is an immediate difficulty. Scripture has not been part of the life of discipleship for Catholics. It is often remarked how, traditionally, Catholics had the sacraments and Protestants had the Bible. Catholics did not read the Bible. There may have been one in the house, but it was untouched. In the past it figured minimally in the training of priests. It is all quite extraordinary when we think about it.

The Reformation encouraged people to read the Bible, and to trust in the authority of their own interpretation. But in Catholic circles there has been a suspicion of this personal reading. The culture has been one of the church leadership directing people in their thinking. So today the Bible remains an unfamiliar book for most people, inhospitable, remote and hard to access. We can see this in how people experience the Liturgy of the Word at Mass.

*The word*
We were conditioned in the past to see the Eucharist in terms of the consecration. To put it crudely, the consecration was the Mass, the rest was trimmings (especially when it was in Latin anyway). But the mindset has been changing and the scripture element of the celebration has a new prominence. Let us look at it from the perspective of Jesus' words: 'Do this in memory of me.'

We gather to remember him who means so much to us. We recall and retell and relive the story. In doing so we reconnect with our roots, we reinforce our identity, we revive our inspiration. We, each of us, 're-align' our personal experience of Christianity and discipleship with the original version.

The scripture at Mass is central to this remembering. Thus the church now says that, at the Eucharist, Christians 'partake of the bread of life from the one table of the Word of God and the Body of Christ'.[46] We are familiar with the table of the bread and wine. But we also gather around the table of scripture. And we are nourished at both. The Word of God is the bread of life also!

Long ago Augustine played with the same symbolism when preaching about the meaning of 'Give us this day our daily bread' in the Our Father:

> Our daily food on this earth is the word of God, which is always being served up in the churches ... The word of God, which is opened up for you every day, and in a manner of speaking broken for you, is daily bread.[47]

We could speak of the 'sacrament of the word'. The real presence of Christ applies to the word no less than to the bread and wine. We say: 'This is the Word of the Lord' and we say: 'This is the Body of Christ'. The two are on a par; in both something divine is happening.

But it does not stop here. The listening needs to be prolonged, to carry over into the days of our week. Discipleship invites us to make the reading of scripture a frequent, familiar activity. The communal reading and listening at Mass is to be complemented by our personal reading, one feeding into the other. Once again, discipleship is both communal and individual.

And if there is no such interaction with scripture? Then our following of Christ may drift into our own reduced, pared-down version of discipleship. Without scripture we may construct a version of discipleship that we are comfortable with rather than challenged by. Reading scripture puts us back in touch with the original challenge.

Every Christian is called to be 'a fifth gospel'. Each of the four gospels tells the story of Jesus in a different way. We read the Bible so that we will be formed in discipleship. Our reading is to help us become another, original, authentic version of the good news. And we do this with others in mind. Someone said: Be careful how you live, you may be the only gospel some people will ever read.

### What is the Bible?
The Bible is an imposing book. It is longer than Tolstoy's *War and Peace*. And at least *War and Peace* is one book; the Bible has over seventy different units, parts of it thousands of years old.

How on earth do we start to deal with it? Starting on page one may not be the best idea.

For Christians, the heart of the Bible is the story of Jesus Christ. Resurrection is the pivotal point, everything else leads into or flows out from this. Following from this event, the Christian movement spread north towards modern-day Turkey and west into Greece and beyond. The Acts of the Apostles tells this part of the story.

Paul is the key figure in the expansion. His letters are the first Christian writings. They are written for the newly-founded Christian communities, to encourage them and help them respond to practical issues. They convey the experience of the earliest Christians and they make for an ever maturing reflection on the meaning of Christianity.

At the same time, oral tradition carries along the story of Jesus' life, death and resurrection. About forty years into the movement, from around 70-100 AD, what we know as the four gospels were written down, finalised. They are four different 'editions' of this oral tradition, each addressed to a different set of circumstances, depending on where and for whom each author was writing.

All this makes up the New Testament. Behind it are what Christians call the Old Testament, the Jewish scriptures (about 80% of our Bible). They were Jesus' own scriptures. So Christians see them as their own pre-history, the environment from which Christianity emerged. Christians read them, not as an interesting antiquity, but because they find there much about themselves and their own faith.

*Inspiration*

The gospels are the place to start, but it is important to appreciate just what we are reading. The gospels are not reporting. If they were, they could have been written forty years earlier, 'on the trail' of Jesus' earthly travels. They are not blow-by-blow accounts. They are not simply to be taken at face value and read literally. There are two reasons for this.

Firstly, the gospels came forty years later. That means forty years of absorbing the experience; reflecting, sifting, interpreting, formulating. It is similar to somebody's biography being written soon after their death and its being written half-a-century later. The one written soon after will have lots of accurate detail. But the later one will have perspective. The gospels resemble the latter. They are very developed reflections, with a great deal of interpretation, a great deal of perspective.

Secondly, the gospels are written from the pivotal point of resurrection. That experience generated the confession of Jesus as 'Lord', as 'Son of God'. So the writers are not simply recalling and interpreting past events, as a biography might. They are testifying. They tell the story of Jesus as testimony. They are not informing us of what he did; they are conveying to us who he is. For them it is a present experience, not a past event.

This makes the gospels a peculiar genre of literature, a complex mix of the historical and the confessional. The four authors choose different events from the tradition in order to communicate their 'angle'. Stories and sayings are edited, embellished, even invented, in order to speak to their own contemporary situations and the issues confronting their Christian communities.

To read the gospels is a corresponding mix of believing and disbelieving. As an historical account of what actually happened, they have a solid core. But they are factually reliable only up to a point. Consulting scripture scholarship helps us negotiate this. But the focus of the gospels is not on the factual. The focus is on communicating who Jesus is. The authors are speaking from their faith to ours.

In the history of literature, the Bible has the status of a classic. For Christians it also has the status of being inspired. What does that mean? Caravaggio has a beautiful painting of Matthew composing his gospel and looking up at the angel hovering over his shoulder. Is that what inspiration is?

Inspiration could be understood crudely, as if the authors were mere puppets and that everything they wrote was intended and approved by God. If that were so, then we would glorify war and wives would be subject to their husbands! Rather, the books of the Bible are human compositions. They are time-conditioned and culture-conditioned. There is much that we today are more enlightened about. And yet this literature is inspired.

I recall seeing a ninth century painting of the evangelist sitting at his bureau. There was no angel, but there was awe in his features. Awe was what he felt in the presence of what he was writing. He was in the presence of inspiration. This was what Vatican II was talking about with the 'one table', the real presence of Christ in the word no less than in the bread and wine. When we read the Bible we are in the presence of inspiration.

Inspiration, though, is two-way. The gospel author was not a pawn, being fed what to write. He was active, imaginative, creative, a real person writing for a real situation. Likewise we are not passive. We are real people with real lives and that is where we are coming from. It is not just that the text we read is inspired. It is that the reading is inspired, an inspired interaction between ourselves and the text.

### Spiritual reading

We can read the Bible literally. If it says that Abraham lived to the age of 175 (Genesis 25:7), then that is how old he was. If it says that Jesus preached his sermon on a mount (Matthew 5:1), then that is where it happened – even though Luke says it was on a plain (Luke 6:17). If it says there were two people called Adam and Eve, then so it was.

Literal reading takes the text at face-value: 'What you see is what you get.' But understanding the Bible requires more than taking it literally. It is not a newspaper and the genre is not reporting. Of course there is a bedrock of what happened. But there is a lot of poetic language. There is a lot of metaphor. And there is a lot of testimony, where historical material is shaped into a confession of faith.

We can also read the Bible allegorically. Here, there are deeper symbolic meanings to be discerned. Take, for example, how the early Christians interpreted the parable of the Good Samaritan. 'The whole human race is that man who was lying on the road … In the Samaritan the Lord Jesus Christ wanted us to understand himself.'[48]

Such interpretations are helpful, even if not intended by the author. But this way of reading can get carried away, as another example from Augustine shows. When Jesus encounters Nathaniel under the fig tree (John 1:48): 'What Jesus sees is the whole human race; what the fig tree stands for is sin'[49] (harking back to Adam's fig leaf). We can end up putting fanciful, subjective meanings into the text.

Then there is a scholarly way of reading scripture. In the case of a gospel, for instance, scholarship informs us about the background and context. We find out when it was written and for whom and why. We learn about the author's style and viewpoint, and his intended meanings in different passages. We discover about the layers in the text and the genesis of the final edition. We distinguish between what goes back to Jesus and what is later embellishment or addition.

All of these ways of reading feed into what is called the spiritual reading of the Bible. We do not have to be scholars, though our reading will benefit from scholarship. We are doing more than taking the words literally. And we are doing more than just reading our own meanings into the text.

Spiritual reading is like a two-way conversation. In a sense there are two 'texts' – that of the scripture and that of the reader's life. In the conversation that is spiritual reading, each text throws light on the other. The text of scripture illuminates the reader's path, while the reader's life-situation opens up the meaning of scripture.

In one way of expressing this, there is first 'the world behind the text'.[50] This is the world of the author, and the author's intentions. Scholarship can help us to understand this world. Then there is 'the world in front of the text'. This world takes in ourselves, our context, our questions. When we engage with the text in this mode, we are opening ourselves to being transformed by our reading. The text opens up a new world of possibility to us.

In this way of reading the Bible, the process of inspiration is at work. In what follows, I outline two ways of reading the Bible spiritually. One begins from scripture, the other from life. But both are about the inspiring interplay between scripture and life.

*Meditation*
The first of these is known as *lectio divina*, or 'divine reading'. This has been the main form of meditation throughout the Christian tradition; this silent, contemplative reading of the Bible. It may be practised alone or in a group. The sequence of steps is from quiet prayer to reading, then to meditating, then to prayer and to contemplation.

Let us say that we choose to meditate on a gospel passage, such as the coming Sunday's gospel. We approach the text with the disposition that God is going to address us. We begin by praying for awareness of the power the words carry. In a mood of prayer we open ourselves to discovering God and discovering ourselves.

Then we read. Whereas a lot of reading today is scanning, speed-reading, looking for quick information, this reading is slow, it is meditative. It pauses to dwell on details, on words and phrases and images. It goes back to read again. Gradually we are opening ourselves to what the words may offer. We are opening ourselves to being surprised.

Thus the reading leads into meditation. Here we allow the text to speak its message and meaning. We allow ourselves to presume that there is a sense in which this text was written especially 'for me'. So we listen as if looking in a mirror. The peculiar genre of the gospels is of relevance here.

Take for instance Jesus and the Samaritan woman (John 4). We are not reading an historical report, as if this is exactly what unfolded. The encounter is related to us from a resurrection perspective. So we are reading of an encounter between the woman and the Lord. This makes it easier to read ourselves into the story. The story is now a template for any Christian to enter into the encounter. Each of us is that woman.

Meditation leads into prayer. God has been addressing us and now we respond. Initially it may be a prayer of thanks for this time of revelation. It may move into a prayer of petition, or of contrition, or of hope. And finally it moves into contemplation, a final moment of stillness and adoration, quietly resting in God.

*Spiritual reflection*

The second way is to begin with our own life and then to read scripture. It sometimes goes by the off-putting name of 'theological reflection', so I have chosen to call it spiritual reflection instead. The sequence is to begin, after quiet prayer, with a reflection on something in our life, then enter into a dialogue between this and a scripture passage, then to conclude with prayer.

A line from T.S. Eliot captures the idea: 'We had the experience, but missed the meaning.'[51] Much of our living is relentless, dictated by the tyranny of the next thing. We are always pushing on. In the process we are failing to notice God's presence. So often God is there but we are gone. But if we return to the experience and meditate on it, it can actually become a different, deeper experience.

After a quiet moment, we begin by choosing something specific from our life to reflect upon. Usually it would be something recent, but not yet 'closed' or fully grasped, something personal and important to us. It might be, for instance, a relationship issue or an incident that was upsetting or some struggle that we are having within ourselves.

We 'replay the tape' of the chosen experience: who? what? where? We connect with our feelings around the occasion. But we do not try to judge or to solve, only to re-evoke. Then we delve deeper. We ask ourselves what was really at issue, what was the underlying question. Perhaps it was something about ourselves, or about life, or about God. We try to get to the heart of the experience

This leads us into the second moment, the dialogue with scripture. The idea is to find an echo of the experience in some scripture passage or story or saying. This is harder or easier, depending on how familiar we are with the Bible. We engage in a dialogue between the scripture and the experience. This is not in order to find a solution; it is two-way. We allow the scripture to illuminate the experience; and we allow our experience to throw light on the scripture.

Finally, in prayer, we bring what has happened to God. Perhaps it is a new insight into ourselves or our situation or God. Perhaps it is something to do. Perhaps little or nothing has emerged; there is no 'result' as yet. But the process can continue and we can return to the reflection. And we give thanks and rest in God.

*For reflection*
Try each of the two approaches outlined above. Devote fifteen to thirty minutes in each case. Reflect on the possibilities each offers you in your spiritual life.

## CHAPTER TWENTY-SIX

# *Conversion and Sin*

It would be hard it to imagine a discussion of Christian life that did not include sin. But in this chapter I want to present the topic in the context of a positive image of Christian living. Our Christian life is our progressing forward into fuller being. I will also discuss the relevance of 'going to confession' in relation to this.

In the past sin was very prominent. Perhaps it was the most prominent aspect of Christian life, at least for Catholics. It was almost as if the spiritual life was a matter of avoiding sin, a kind of spiritual obstacle course. And more likely than not, sin was about sex. Sexuality, it seemed, was where we are most susceptible to the power of sin.

It was all quite negative. It was as if there was a cloud of guilt hanging permanently over us, like the rain over the bog. People could not trust themselves and neither could the church. The church sought to restrain people, suppressing their inclinations with commandments and sanctions. And God was conceived in the image of this church, as a God who looked down sternly on people.

### Conversion

I want to use the term 'conversion' to convey a positive view of our Christian living. The word means different things to people. It can mean St Paul on his horse; it can be about evangelising; it can be about currency exchange. Here I am thinking of the literal meaning of the word, which has to do with turning. My image of Christian life is of a 'turning towards'.

The Greek word used in the gospels is *metanoia*. Usually translated as 'repent', it has the sense of a change of mindset, the turning of our mindset in a different direction. The followers of Jesus are called to a change in the orientation of their seeing, of their feeling, and ultimately of their choices. There is to be a new focus for their attention and, as a result, of their energy. As the phrase has it, 'where attention goes, energy flows'.

Conversion is central to the Christian calling. Jesus' first

words in Mark's gospel are: 'The time is fulfilled and the kingdom of God has come near; repent and believe in the good
news' (Mark 1:15). Later, when Peter proclaims that the risen
Jesus is Lord and Messiah, and people ask what they are to do,
he continues: 'Repent and be baptised in the name of Jesus
Christ' (Acts 2:38).

The order of thoughts is crucial; conversion comes second. A
lot of our conditioning has led us to think it comes first; if I repent, then I will be forgiven. It is 'if, then' thinking. Forgiveness
comes to seem conditional. But in fact the order is the other way
around. It is not 'if, then' but 'because, therefore'. Because the
kingdom of God has come near, because Jesus is Lord, because
you are loved – therefore be converted.

This is the same conditioning that allows sin to put itself to
the fore. When sin takes over the driving seat, we think: 'I have
sinned; if I confess I will be forgiven.' Or: 'We are born into sin,
so we have to be baptised.' Or: 'Original sin set the world off
beam, so God had to come to our rescue.' In each case sin sets
the agenda. It is the 'Plan B' thinking we spoke of.

But it is grace that is first; God's self-sharing in the very act of
creation, in the daily miracle of creation, in the Incarnation.
Because of sin, we experience this as a forgiving, reconciling,
justifying grace. But the grace is first. First up is that each of us is
graced, embraced, rejoiced-in by God. The challenge to us, in
our fragility, is to see ourselves thus, to allow ourselves be
drawn into this light.

Conversion is our response. And its mood is joy.
'Repentance' can suggest a mood of sackcloth and ashes, but the
predominant mood has to be one of joy. We are being presented
with good news, about ourselves, our world, our lives. In response,
our life is a turning towards. We allow ourselves to be drawn towards the one who comes near, to be drawn to the light, into
hope, into this path of possibility.

Recall the story of Jesus with the woman who committed
adultery (John 8). Where her accusers define her by her sin,
Jesus sees her future, her possibility. He draws her towards the
light. His attitude to her is totally positive. In his eyes 'a new creation is everything' (Galatians 6:15). This is God's first word to
us, challenging us to believe in our capacity to be transformed.

*What is sin?*

The word 'sin' needs some untangling. It is commonly thought to mean what is forbidden by the church; for example, missing Mass or using contraceptives or stealing from others. Already here we can see a common denominator; sin is being cast as disobedience. Yet the three examples are significantly dissimilar.

Missing Mass, whatever might be wrong about it, is an intra-church thing. It only applies to Catholics. Stealing, though, is in the realm of what is right or wrong for anybody. It is in the realm of what makes us more human or less human, whereas Mass is about being more Catholic or less Catholic. And contraception? Which of the two it is more like has been a subject of much debate.

Staying with the example of stealing, let us call it 'wrong' rather than sin. Its wrongness lies, not in its being forbidden, but in how we see ourselves as human beings. It is wrong because it goes against what befits us as persons. It works against our personal and social becoming. It causes suffering to others and harm to ourselves.

The word 'sin' adds something further. It is a theological word, that is, a word that Christians use to express how they see their wrongdoings. When they do wrong it is, by and large, the same wrongdoing as anybody else. But they experience it also as against the gospel, a turning away from the path of discipleship. It is the opposite of conversion; it is 'aversion'.

Two examples will illustrate this graphically (even if they come from the Old Testament). One is the story of king David and Bathsheba (2 Samuel 11-12). The king seduces Bathsheba, but she becomes pregnant. Eager to cover up, he recalls her husband Uriah from the battlefront, to wine and dine him. But he will not sleep with his wife while his army is at war. Desperate, David has Uriah put in the front line of battle and he is duly killed. After the mourning he takes Bathsheba as his wife and a son is born to the king.

The other is the story of king Ahab and Naboth (1 Kings 21). Naboth's vineyard borders on the king's and Ahab offers a good deal in order to acquire it. But Naboth is loath to part with what is the family inheritance. While Ahab sulks, his wife Jezebel contrives to have Naboth falsely accused of blaspheming, for which he is duly executed, according to the law. After an appropriate period, Ahab takes the vineyard.

These stories evoke strong feelings. It is appalling how the powerful trample on the defenceless in pursuit of their unchecked desires. It is shocking how the whole affair is covered up so that nobody is any the wiser. Worse still, people actually believe that a soldier has died bravely for his people and that a blasphemer has been fairly punished. It was always thus.

But look at how many of the 'ten commandments' have been broken. You shall not kill; you shall not commit adultery; you shall not steal; you shall not bear false witness against your neighbour; you shall not covet your neighbour's wife; you shall not covet your neighbour's goods. It is quite impressive.

It could hardly be clearer that morality is about much more than obeying or breaking rules. It is about right relationships between people, relationships that are person-making rather than person-breaking. It is about the underlying sense of integrity and responsibility and fidelity and self-discipline. Rules like the ten commandments are only shorthand for this.

Now to sin. Both stories have a 'part two', where the prophet comes on the scene; Nathan in the case of David, Elijah in the case of Ahab. Essentially each says to the king: 'In doing this you have broken covenant with God' (which is the focus of the first three commandments). In doing wrong, they have turned away instead of being drawn towards the light. They have not just done wrong; they have sinned.

So, sin is not a special category of wrongs that Christians commit. There is a universal meaning of wrongdoing; that which causes suffering, which tears at solidarity and right relationships, which makes us less human. Sin is how Christians understand their wrongdoing. They understand it as aversion from the drawing power of grace.

### Mortal sin

Theology differentiates between what it calls mortal and venial sin. Past usage gave the impression that people were frequently guilty of committing mortal sins. Views have moved on.

The word 'mortal' means deadly. Mortal sin is about decisive moves along the path of 'aversion'. In a non-religious context, it would correspond to a person's betrayal of all that it means to be a human being, their alienation from themselves. In a Christian context, this is understood to signify also the death of a relationship, the person's alienation from the God of Jesus Christ.

The term 'mortal sin' sounds like an single action. But it should be obvious that what we are describing here is the state a person ends up in as a result of their actions. Mortal sin is this state. It is something momentous in a person's life, a state of fundamental spiritual alienation. That is rare, not frequent. It is most likely about a pattern of action than any single act, a pattern of adult choices that take a person in a definitive direction.

'Venial sin' is defined as the daily failings we are all liable to. Here we are talking about individual actions. They vary in their gravity or seriousness, according to what is happening the person. But such acts can form patterns. And the pattern can ultimately amount to a changed orientation in a person's life. We see here the ambiguity of the word 'sin'. Is it about an action or about a person? In fact it is about both.

*Discernment*
The key issue is discernment. The key is learning to discern well where our choices are taking us, to identify the impact of how we act on who we are. This discernment has traditionally been called our 'examination of conscience'. But it is not about going through a checklist like the ten commandments. It is more like an expansion of consciousness, our sensitising ourselves to the significance of own living.

Discernment is about becoming more sensitised on a number of fronts. First, we are becoming sensitised to our own actions. We become aware of what they are doing to others and what they are doing to ourselves. We are growing in awareness of the good or suffering we are causing to ourselves and to others.

We are also being sensitised to our own inner selves. We are getting in touch with the 'jungle' of what is within us. We are familiarising ourselves with our desires, motivations, needs, biases, drives. This is where our actions stem from. And it is a jungle. A lot of the time we would not be able to fully explain why we did what we did. One reflection put it as follows:

> Below the surface stream, shallow and light of what we
> say and feel … below the stream the light of what we think
> we feel, there flows with noiseless current, strong obscure
> and deep the central stream of what we feel indeed.[52]

Here we encounter our potential for self-deception, as well as
our own lack of true freedom. Discernment here is about growing in self-knowledge.

Discernment is also about our social context. We alert ourselves to the ways in which our society influences how we think
about what we do. 'Societies' would be more accurate, for we each
belong to different groups or sub-cultures. We are all getting different messages as to what human fullness consists in, as to what
path we should follow. We seek to become critically aware of these
different voices and of the attractions and pressures they exert.

Finally, discernment happens on a specifically spiritual level.
Here we are being sensitised to what is happening us on the
path of discipleship. We are reviewing our progress or otherwise in turning towards the one who is drawing us into grace.

The role I see for the church is to be of help to people as they
discern. Its role used to be one of telling people what to do, promoting obedience and conformity rather than freedom. Its role
today is one of encouraging sensitivity, encouraging people to
grow in the exercise of their own conscience. Its role is to facilitate discernment. Maybe it could be a kind of forum for the kind
of conversations that would help people become more discerning on these different fronts.

*Going to confession*
What, finally, about going to confession? Today it is usually
called the Sacrament of Reconciliation, itself a reflection of the
new emphasis on forgiveness over sin. Still, people ask: 'Isn't it
enough to confess to God?' The more fundamental question,
though, is whether there is a future for the sacrament.

What Catholics are used to is a private devotional practice,
between an individual and a priest. The impression used to be
that this was prerequisite to going to Communion. Notice the
mindset here. First, we are back in a privatised version of discipleship (me and the priest). Second, sin is back in the driving
seat setting the agenda ('if confession, then communion').

It is worth noting that it has always been the understanding in Christianity that there are different ways of accessing God's forgiveness; that is, apart from the sacrament. They include participation in the Eucharist, prayer, acts of kindness and, notably, our forgiving others when we are wronged. These are the ordinary, normal ways in which Christians experience forgiveness.

The sacrament has been seen as necessary only for 'serious' wrongs. In the early church this referred to a small number of very grave actions whereby a person effectively excommunicated themselves. Then there was needed a process of reconciliation with the community which included a 'course' of penance. Today there is a lack of clarity here, with the words 'serious' and 'mortal' often used loosely.

The future of the sacrament might be along the following lines. What comes first is a life of conversion, allowing ourselves to be drawn by the light. Driving this is our daily prayer and discernment. It is also characterised by our practising 'the ministry of reconciliation' (2 Corinthians 5:18). In our relationships we learn to forgive and to allow ourselves be forgiven. All this is our daily practice of what the sacrament is all about.

Next, we participate in the Eucharist. Listen to its prayers: 'May almighty God have mercy on us, forgive us our sins'; 'This is the cup of my blood, shed so that sins may be forgiven'; 'This sacrament which has made our peace with you'; 'Lamb of God, you take away the sins of the world'; 'Only say the word and I shall be healed'. The Eucharist is the great sacrament of reconciliation, our primary communal celebration of forgiveness.

Within this framework, we can situate a specific 'sacrament of reconciliation'. It would, first and foremost, be a communal event, for that is what each sacraments is. It would be a gathering. To it we would bring our daily experiences of conversion and reconciliation. We would do so in order to celebrate the grace of forgiveness already at work in our lives, in the 'sacrament' of our daily life.

This would be different from what is there now. We have a communal liturgy (known as 'Rite 2') which has done a lot of good. But it is an abbreviated form of individual confession to a priest, within a communal setting. What I am suggesting would be more like what is known as 'Rite 3', which is a general absolution, and which is rarely permitted. The focus there is on a communal celebration of forgiveness, with no individual confession.

What we know traditionally as 'going to confession' would have a smaller place. 'Confession is good for the soul.' It involves going individually to a priest, as representing the community we have failed in our sin. But it could mean talking with a trusted friend and experiencing God's forgiving grace in that. Or it might involve going to the one we hurt, and seeing that person also as a minister of reconciliation.

*For reflection*
How has your own understanding of sin changed over the years?

CHAPTER TWENTY-SEVEN

## *Loving the World*

It sometimes seems that previous generations were more focused on heaven than earth, on their entry into the next world than their life in this one. So now we ask; what is the attitude of Christianity towards this world? How does the church see its role in the world? Here we will be developing what was said above about vocation and mission.

### The main thing

I begin with another question. What is the main thing 'bothering' the church? I mean, what is its preoccupation, its main concern? What are its thoughts taken up with? Maybe the answer varies with different times and circumstances.

There will be one answer if the church is an 'approved of' body in society, well thought of and looked up to. There will be another if it is a marginal group, lacking prestige, not taken seriously. In the former case its concern might be just to keep things ticking over and running smoothly. In the latter it might be more concerned with reaching out and marketing its message.

Again, its concerns might be different if it is a powerful force in society than if it is discredited. A powerful church might be interested in expanding its power, as well as protecting its power. It might be interested in control. A discredited church would be humbler, perhaps concerned with looking critically at itself and reforming. Maybe as well, these things go in cycles.

Another way of asking the question is: what is the main thing bothering the individual Christian, in their capacity as a Christian? Obviously it would include the issues in their own life at a given time: family, work, and so on. But in some fashion what bothers the individual will be what bothers the church. For, if we are a community of disciples, then we have a common concern or preoccupation. Otherwise the church is 'out there'.

But it is a third question that brings us to the answer. What is the main thing bothering God? What is God's main concern, God's preoccupation? For the essence of what the church is all about is that it is meant to be immersed in what preoccupies

God. It focuses on what God is focused on. I am not speculating here about 'God' in general, but asking about the very specific God whose self-portrait is Jesus of Nazareth.

### God's concern

What preoccupies the God of Jesus Christ is the world. Creation, the evolving universe, is God's baby, as it were. And the essence of this world is what God dreams for it. Its 'soul' is its potential to become fully itself. The God who comes near to us in Jesus is not primarily interested in God's own self. This God's primary interest is God's world and how God's people are with one another in God's world. That is God's passion. That would be God's glory. 'God so loved the world ...' (John 3:16).

So God rejoices when God's world evolves in this direction and when women and men live in this spirit. God rejoices when relationships are lived by values of truth and peace and justice, between people, between peoples, and between people and their environment. For that is when the world becomes a better place, more like God's dream in creating it. On the other hand, God mourns at the opposite of this. God mourns at suffering in the world, and at the sin that causes most of the world's suffering. God mourns when God's dream for the world is frustrated.

This is the God portrayed in Jesus. 'Kingdom', the main theme of Jesus' life, is his word for God's dream. Kingdom means the future of the world, its inner reality. It is focused especially on the woundedness and pain of the world. Jesus, in his compassion and solidarity, is the mouthpiece of this pain. This is captured eloquently in the poem 'The Kingdom' by the Welsh poet R. S. Thomas:

> It's a long way off but inside it
> There are quite different things going on:
> Festivals at which the poor man
> Is king and the consumptive is
> Healed; mirrors in which the blind look
> At themselves and love looks at them
> Back; and industry is for mending
> The bent bones and the minds fractured
> By life. It's a long way off, but to get
> There takes no time and admission

Is free, if you will purge yourself
Of desire, and present yourself with
Your need only and the simple offering
Of your faith, green as a leaf.

So, this is what should preoccupy the church, namely, God's world, which is God's kingdom, God's work-in-progress. This is what the church exists for. The church is 'ordained' for the world. It exists, not for itself, but for the sake of the world, to be at the service of creation becoming fully itself. It is ordained into existence to collaborate in God's great work.

(The above is not intended to be exclusivist. Any religion should have this sense of itself. Every human being should feel part of this divine project. But Christianity and Christian churches come at it out of their own specific revelation and worldview and inspiration.)

*Loving the world*
This means that Christianity is called to love the world. But it is possible to get love wrong. Preoccupations can be misguided. It is possible to fall in love with the world, in the sense of its allure, thereby forgetting the kingdom. It is possible for the church to become 'worldly' in a bad sense. The church could become pre-occupied with itself rather than the world, with its own growth and survival, with its own prestige or power.

It is also possible for Christianity to get love wrong through a negativity towards the world. It can make too sharp an opposition between 'this world' and 'the next world'. Spirituality can see the world as no more than something to suffer and endure on the way to the next. For example, this is what is implied sometimes at a funeral when people say of the person who died, 'their sufferings are over'.

Such negativity may also see the world as the place of sin, as essentially corrupt and corrupting. Either way, it makes for an otherworldly focus, for a flight from the world. This is reflected in how we used the word 'heaven' or the phrase 'saving my soul'. It makes for a religion that is separate from life, where the concerns of religion are not the concerns of daily life. The world is not loved: it is feared, or it is disdained, but it is not a friend.

Suffering and sin are a big part of life in the world. But a lop-sided emphasis misses the grace, that fundamental sense of the world as good because it is from God. In a balanced outlook, the world is to be both affirmed and critiqued. It is affirmed for what it is and critiqued for its losing sight of its calling. It is critiqued for the sake of itself, not because it is seen as evil.

The Vatican II document on the church in today's world expresses the spirit of how Christianity loves the world. It brings this world and the beyond into a single focus and a single sense of appreciation:

> The expectation of a new earth increases rather than diminishes our concern for developing this one. For here the body of a new human family grows, foreshadowing the age which is to come. That is why earthly progress is of vital concern to the kingdom of God. When we have nurtured on earth the values of human dignity, solidarity and freedom, we will find them again, but freed of stain, illuminated and transfigured. Here on earth the kingdom is mysteriously present; when the Lord comes, it will be brought to its full perfection.[53]

What, then, does Christianity or the church wish for the world and for God's people living in the world? Many have the impression that all the church wishes is for itself; for people to 'join us'. Many feel that the church is saying: 'You need to join us if you want to be saved.' Of course people inside the church think like this too. But that is a self-centred thinking, a church preoccupied with itself.

Rather, the church's wish for the world is Jesus' prayer: 'Thy will be done, thy kingdom come.' Its wish is that God's glory would shine in the world. It wishes, in the words of Jesus, that people would have life and have it to the full (John 10:10). For that is God's glory. The glory of God is when God's dream for the world comes true.

That is the church's primary wish for the world. The church also wishes that the world would know Jesus. To know him is to encounter in 'self-portrait' the source and giver of the grace that is life in the world. If people come to know Jesus they may also want to be part of the community that celebrates his coming. So any wish for people to 'join us' is not self-centred. It is God-centred, world-centred, people-centred.

*World-loving holiness*

Let us turn now to the individual Christian. How is he or she caught up in Christianity's love for the world, in God's passion for the world? How does it work out practically in the spirituality and the existence of the believer?

First, it involves each of us overcoming in ourselves the kind of temptations already outlined. Faith can be 'for me' rather than 'for the world'. It can be otherworldly, about 'heaven' and not about 'kingdom'. Or our real love may be worldly advancement, where the gospel is professed but other values are lived.

A true love for the world is what we call holiness. The chapter on vocation described holiness as making faith real, integrating faith and life. It is when an intense sense of God coincides with an intense sense of the world. Real holiness is not divorced from reality. It is socially-conscious; it is a mysticism attuned to the world. It is a passion for the world, a compassion for the other, a solidarity with suffering. And this is at the same time an intense experience of God.

Latin American Christianity gave us the term 'preferential option for the poor', to convey this world-loving form of holiness. This preferential option means that attention is directed to where need is greatest. As somebody put it, it is a mysticism 'with open eyes'. Faith, guided by compassion leads us to see more and not less. It leads us to see the world as God sees and to feel as God feels.

This world-loving holiness also goes further than compassion. Recall Jesus' compassion and how its reverse side was criticism. Love for the world mourns over all that frustrates the world's becoming. It is angry at the suffering. It asks, why? It asks, what kind of world allows this? It looks for the causes and for the underlying sin in society. The holiness that loves the world also questions the world.

The church has engaged in a lot of analysis about poverty and injustice, about peace and violence, about suffering and its causes. It has come out with much that is prophetic, a resource for believers in understanding what is going on in the world. But this has often gone unnoticed, with all the attention its pronouncements on sexual ethics have attracted. As a result, its vision of justice in the world has been called its best kept secret.

Holiness, I am saying, is political as well as spiritual. By 'political' I mean taking sides. Both the church and the individual have to take sides. Compassion leads into criticism and criticism leads to naming causes and identifying sources. If this does not entail taking sides, it remains at the level of agreeable sentiments and platitudes.

Taking sides is meant, not in the sense of party politics, but in the sense of a preferential option for the poor. It is taking the side of the victim, the downtrodden. It is looking at reality from where they stand. But it may also mean changing sides. For the downtrodden can become the oppressor, as W.B. Yeats observed in his poem 'The Great Day':

Hurrah for revolution and more cannon-shot!
A beggar upon horseback lashes a beggar on foot.
Hurrah for revolution and cannon come again!
The beggars have changed places, but the lash goes on.

*Parish*
Christians exercise world-loving holiness in different ways. It could be as part of a church organisation such as the St Vincent de Paul Society. It could be as part of a social action group where they work alongside others who come from other inspirations, but with the same passion for the world. It could be a community involvement, making the world a better place locally. It could be something quiet, unseen, but no less real.

But one thing that all Christians share in is the local worshipping community – usually a parish in this part of the world. I recall a discussion at one parish meeting about the meaning of 'parish'. The way one person expressed it was: 'We care that you exist.' It captures very well the world-loving holiness of the parish community. Parish is meant to be this experience.

In the local 'world' of each parish, alongside the joys of life, there is much struggle and pain, often silent and borne alone. The challenge is that all people would have a strong sense that 'We care that you exist.' They would know that, in this place in the world at least, they are noticed and they matter. Each time Eucharist is celebrated, they would know that their joys and pains are brought to the altar.

In its own locality, each Christian community is called to be all that 'church' is. It is meant to share God's preoccupation. Each parish is to be a place where God's passion is 'earthed', made real for this particular place and time. When parish is like this, it puts flesh on God's love for the world. Incarnation becomes here, it becomes now.

*For reflection*
'World-loving holiness'; what does it mean and what do you think of it?

CHAPTER TWENTY-EIGHT

# Spirituality and Sexuality

The last chapter spoke about holiness as loving the world. But it is not obvious that Christianity invites us to love our sexuality. Here I want to suggest how Christianity invites us to see a positive relationship between our spirituality and our sexuality.

I am aware that, against the background of the clerical child abuse uncovered, anything the Catholic church says about sexuality has been discredited. Maybe its traditional approach to sexuality is part of the problem. All the more important, then, to see if there is a positive, helpful Christian vision of sexuality to be articulated.

I also want to mention some of the controversial areas – homosexuality, contraception, sex apart from marriage, people in second relationships. What I will say is extremely brief. But I would like to find a meeting point, or a point of reconciliation, between what the church says and the lived experience of men and women. This involves seeing where the church is coming from and it involves listening to what is happening today.

## Suffering
There is a view that the church should stay out of sexuality. I do not think that it should stay out of the area completely, but it should retire from the micro-managing of people's lives and focus more on what really matters.

In this regard, what stands out for me is the association between sexuality and suffering. The last chapter was about Christianity loving the world, concerned above all else with what is happening God's people in God's world. This makes for a heightened attention to suffering. Yet, when we think about it, there is an extraordinary amount of suffering that is bound up with sexuality. Let me illustrate.

Much suffering is caused by sexual violence: rape, abuse, trafficking, as well as the damage done to people by pornography. There is suffering and trauma connected with abortion. There is the suffering of a broken marriage, of a deserted partner, of a single parent. There is the suffering of a marriage that is a living nightmare.

There is the suffering of a couple who are infertile. There is the suffering of a couple who are struggling with planning a family. There is the suffering of the homosexual person, the self-discovery, the isolation, the social reactions. There is the suffering of women in a patriarchal culture. There is the sexual suffering of people living with a disability. And there is the pain and struggle of just growing up sexually.

The confusion of our society about sexuality also makes for suffering. In a more traditional society sex had its place and its place was procreation. In recent times contraception has liberated sex as it were, so that it can be about something else. Is it about love? Is it about having babies? Is it about having fun? Is it casual or serious? Is it a commodity or a treasure?

The point here is that our sexuality is socially constructed. Our ideas about our sexuality, what it is and what it is for, do not just come from ourselves. The society we live in is a powerful voice (or collection of voices), telling us how to think. What counts as success, as happiness? What does 'being good at sex' really mean? What are the values that matter? The confusion can be quite troubling; another, less apparent source of suffering.

*Part of the problem?*
Previous chapters have presented the vision of a church of compassion, that cares that we exist and how we exist, a church that is critical of the sin that causes suffering. But now a question arises. If there is a lot of suffering associated with sexuality, has the church also been a cause of suffering? I am not talking about child abuse here, but of other issues where the answer may not be as obvious.

There is something unhealthy about the way the church has been involved in trying to manage people's sexual lives. It has sent a message to people that, when it comes to sex, you have to be perfect before you begin. Its severe stance has made for a great deal of shame and guilt and pain in what should be a journey of joyful discovery.

Again, the church's approach to specific issues – leaving aside the rights and wrongs of the teachings – has not been compassionate. It has been experienced as judgemental, even condemning. Very many have felt excluded over abortion, over infertility, over homosexuality, over a second relationship, over birth control. Many find it hard to believe that 'we care that you exist'. They feel that they have no place at the table.

It is disturbing to contrast the attention given by the church in recent decades to contraception on the one hand and to sexual violence on the other. The church appears to be more interested in the world of family planning than in the world of sexual exploitation. That seems to be coming out of something other than a concern about suffering.

Going back in history, we find a tradition of negativity about sex and sexuality. (The negativity, though, is not confined to Christianity, nor does it originate there.) From its early centuries, when practices of sexual renunciation evolved, Christianity developed a sense of sexuality as the weak-point in humanity, the point most susceptible to moral corruption. This linked in with thinking about original sin. It had corrupted sexuality; it was even thought to be transmitted through sexual intercourse.

In this mentality the only justification for sex was procreation. Overall, though, sexuality was an obstacle. Sexuality and spirituality were enemies. It could not be imagined how sexual experience and sexual activity could contribute to the growth of a person's spiritual self. Spiritual growth came through the denial of the sexual and through sexual abstinence.

So we find that, until recently it was the Catholic tradition that virginity was a higher state than marriage. We find it still the case that, for many, 'sin' and 'sex' are synonymous. All this, of course, is also a social construction of our sexuality, a way of thinking impressed on us from outside. And it has caused great suffering.

### Part of the solution?
In all of this, Christianity has let itself down and failed to do justice to itself. There is something more positive to be unearthed in the Christian tradition. This something more positive is part of the spirit and thrust of the Bible, notwithstanding the patriarchal culture of those times.

Let us start with Genesis, with the words after each day's work of creation: 'God saw that it was good'. On the sixth day, after creating man and woman: 'God saw all that he had made and indeed it was very good'. God's world is good. Sexuality is part of God's good world. Sexuality is good.

One book of the Bible, the Song of Songs, stands out for this message. It is where we get the line: 'love is strong as death' (8:6). The book is a short one, about a man and woman and their love. It is romantic, even erotic: 'O may your breasts be like clusters of the vine ... and your kisses like the best wine that goes down smoothly gliding over lips and teeth' (7:8-9).

Yet, while it is a book of the Bible, it is the only book that never mentions God. This is not because God would not approve. It is more because God does not need to be mentioned. This sexual love is simply a good part of creation. The Bible knows it is good and the writing is full of praise and joy.

Turning to the prophets, they searched for a language with which to talk about God and humanity. The language they found to speak most deeply and eloquently was the language of man and woman. It is the language in creation nearest to what God is like with us and we with God. Thus, for instance, Hosea explores the imagery of marriage (and adultery) to talk about the relationship between God and God's people.

Sexuality is not far from us in the gospels either. Think of the woman who washes Jesus' feet with her tears, dries them with her hair, kisses them with her lips, anoints them with ointment (Luke 7). It is striking how sensuous the description is. And yet it is a moment of salvation, a spiritual encounter.

Or think of Jesus and the woman by the well in Samaria (John 4). There is nobody else there, it is an isolated spot, it is a man and a woman. They are even talking about her sexual history. When the disciples return they 'are astonished that he was speaking with a woman'. And again it is a moment of salvation, an encounter of grace.

Then there is the simple fact of Jesus – his body – the word 'made flesh'. Our central image and symbol is the cross – his body – our salvation. In Christianity we are not saved from the body. We are saved bodily. Salvation is bodily.

These reflections offer a basis for seeing sexuality as gift rather than threat. It is not sinful and a thing of shame. It is not to be glorified into a thing of enslavement. It is gift. To be a sexual being is good, a cause of gratitude. It is a dimension of blessing in our human becoming. It invites us into our deeper self; it is a path of joy and mystery.

Christianity can thus offer an alternative 'construction' of our sexuality. It offers a positive perspective on what it means to be 'good at sex'. It speaks of our sexuality as person-building, part of the respect and love and communion between persons. It sees deep happiness coming in and through our sexuality, and not through bypassing or suppressing it. It sees sexuality and spirituality as friends, our sexual lives as part of our spiritual experience and journey.

In this view the biggest sins in the area of sexuality are about justice. They are when sexual activity is person-breaking and not person-building. The biggest sins are when it causes suffering like that outlined above. This reflects God's passion and preoccupation. The strongest church teachings should be directed at this, in the same spirit of compassion-and-criticism as the last chapter.

*The moral issues*
When we look at the moral issues, it helps to see where the church is coming from. The key point in its position is the intrinsic link it sees between sex, marriage and procreation. To keep these three united, it argues, is the vital factor in protecting what human sexuality is about.

In the past all the church's emphasis was on procreation. More recent thinking has moved on to a more balanced view that appreciates the relationship and not just the procreation. Sexual intercourse, the church now says, has its meaning in the context of the committed relationship we call marriage, a relationship that of its nature is creative and procreative. This is its basis for evaluating a number of moral issues.

Contraceptives are seen as wrong because they exclude procreation. Sexual intercourse is wrong when it is between people who are not married. And homosexual sexual activity is wrong because it is apart from both marriage and procreation. (Artificial forms of conception are wrong because they separate procreation from sexual intercourse, but there are also issues here around the generation of multiple embryos.)

In the last century another way of seeing all this has come

about. The advent of effective contraception makes it possible to
separate sex from any possibility of procreation. Sex has taken
on a new meaning today. It is primarily about relationship. It is
not seen to be linked intrinsically to procreation, or to marriage,
or to heterosexual couples. The church's position has its rationale, but there is also another rationale here, another 'reasonable
vision'.

## Contraception

In the 1960s, following Vatican II, a papal commission was set
up to review church teaching in the context of the new contra-
ceptive developments. There was a widespread expectation of
change. The commission concluded with a majority and a minority
view, the majority in favour of change. But Pope Paul VI went
with the minority view in his document *Humanae Vitae*.

There was agreement about the link between sex, marriage
and procreation. But the commission disagreed about how this
link is held. The majority view spoke in terms of the marriage as
a whole being open to new life. But *Humanae Vitae* demanded
that each and every act of intercourse be open to new life. No
'artificial' obstacle could be put in the way of what was seen as
God's design, God's 'natural law' for sex. In the end, the weight
of a traditional way of thinking was decisive.

The weight of contemporary experience, however, was lean-
ing in another direction and there was no meeting point. The
outcome is that a majority of those who stay with the church follow their own conscience, while the official teaching is increasingly disregarded. It is unable to communicate or to convince,
with its laboured arguments, based on an antiquated version of
natural law philosophy.

## Sex and marriage

Leaving procreation aside, the church's restriction of sexual
intercourse to marriage is out of sync with contemporary experience. Here, though, the church's position may have more going
for it.

It may help if we avoid legalistic arguments that draw a line
between sex that is and sex that is not 'morally legitimate'.
Instead we might think of a spectrum of different contexts in
which sex takes place. At one end of the spectrum is violent and

abusive sex. At the other end is sex within a committed and caring relationship. In between, there is casual sex; and there is sex within a transient or shorter-term relationship.

A legalistic view says, for instance, that an engaged couple having sex is wrong, because it is outside marriage. But thinking of a spectrum of different contexts takes us in a different direction. It allows us to appreciate what is present as much as what is absent. We think now about what is there of the 'ideal' and what is far from ideal. We talk about our different ideals, as well as the ways in which our sexuality is socially constructed.

This also helps identify the important battles to be fought. They are about what is person-building and what is person-breaking. Perhaps the main area for debate today is between sex that is casual and sex that is relational. The main issue may be the trivialisation of sexual encounter. That is where most can be done to 'save' sexuality. But it is not clear that this is where the church is drawing its battle lines.

*Homosexuality*
The church's view of homosexuality is rooted in times when there was no understanding of a homosexual orientation. In those times (which include biblical times) it was presumed that everybody was heterosexual. Therefore what we call homosexual sexual activity was understood to be heterosexual people engaging in perverse actions.

Recent times have left the church struggling. It says that homosexuality is not a sin but that it is a tendency towards actions that are disordered; that it is a disordered sexual inclination. It maintains a distinction between the person and the action and it affirms the dignity of the person. But it is hard for homosexual persons to feel respected alongside such descriptions of their being.

As with contraception, there is a sense that the debate has been lost by the church. Homosexuality needs to be respected simply as sexuality, with the same language of goodness and gift, of person-building and communion and creativity. Questions face the church as to whether its argument is culturally-bound or theologically based.

At the same time, western culture is moving quite quickly;

homosexuality was only decriminalised in Ireland in 1993. It is increasingly seen as 'normal', perhaps in the kind of way that being left-handed is normal. But here again the social construction of sexuality can be quite powerful. It can be just as hard to question social trends as it is to question church teaching. Maybe both church and society are too defensive in the conversation about what sexuality is and about what we do not understand.

In all these areas, for church, there is something to hold on to and something to let go of. There is the possibility of a vision that is spiritually and biblically rooted, that is transformative, that is prophetic – and that is inclusive. But much of what comes across is different, lacking scriptural basis and too unwilling to engage with new thinking.

*Remarriage*

There are strong New Testament grounds for the church's position on divorce – in what Jesus said and in what Paul wrote (although that need not mean it is closed to review). The position is expressed theologically in terms of the relationship between a Christian husband and wife being symbolic of the relationship between Christ and the church; therefore demanding absolute fidelity.

The fact, though, is that marriages break up. People get divorced and remarry civilly, or they move into new relationships. In these situations the church refuses communion because, it says, their situation is an 'objective contradiction' of the meaning of Christian marriage as symbolic of Christ's love for the church. The position has its rationale but it is experienced as exclusive, especially by those who are the victims in broken marriages.

Theologians have been exploring ways forward. These usually involve seeing the situation in a less legalistic way, for instance in terms of healing rather than law. The focus here is on bringing something good from what has happened rather than on judging. From this there emerges a possibility of recognising the second relationship, even if not in quite the same way as the first.

A more radical line of questioning would ask whether a Christian marriage is 'indissoluble' simply by virtue of a contract, or whether it becomes indissoluble (or not) over time. Maybe, in this way of looking at it, there can be the total destruction or 'death' of a relationship that was intended to be indissoluble and which sought for a time to become so.

At the same time, there is what is happening marriage in society. Increasingly it is breaking down, increasingly it is a temporary arrangement. So this is not about the church accommodating itself to a new situation, for that situation is highly unsatisfactory. Rather, it is about the church allowing itself be challenged by an increasingly unsatisfactory situation within the Christian community, among its own members.

*Listening*
The above touches but lightly on very important questions. All I would wish to conclude is that there is unfinished business for the church in its teachings about sexuality. The sheer extent of disagreement is saying something. There is listening to be done.

There is need for listening to the experience and wisdom of married people, of infertile couples, of homosexual people, of separated men and women. There is need for the listening to become a moment in the teaching, for the inner wisdom of people to inform the collective wisdom of the church, and not just *vice versa*.

There is also need for a shift of emphasis, away from moral legalism and towards the issue of how sexuality is socially constructed. The impression is that the church would control the sexual lives of individuals. What it needs to be is a prophetic and inspiring voice in a world that is unclear about what sexuality is.

*For reflection*
Spirituality and sexuality; not enemies but friends. Reflect on what has been your own experience of this.

CHAPTER TWENTY-NINE

## *Belonging is Critical*

Like other organisations, the church has its doctrines and orthodoxies. It expects its people to identify with them. So 'belonging'
includes feeling comfortable around this. But people have di-
verging views and have difficulties with various positions. There
are difficulties, we know, with what the church says about sexuality, about women, about authority, about ecumenism, as well
as with what it says on other less publicised issues.

So where does a person stand when unable to agree? What
level of assent is required in order to belong? Where is a diversity
of views legitimate? Is it possible for a person to be in strong disagreement and still to belong?

*Reconfiguration*
In the first chapter I referred to the shift from 'the experience of
authority' to 'the authority of experience'. For previous generations the experience of church was an experience of authority
and obedience. People were told what to do and what to think.
Conscience was often little more than 'coming around to our
way of thinking'.

It was the clerical church. The hierarchy held the wisdom
and uttered the teachings. 'Laity' had its secular sense of unqualified, deferring to those who knew. One person described it
with a nautical image. The captain up on the deck has a clear
view; the rest of us are like those working down below in the
boiler room, unable to see.

Pope Pius X, writing in the early twentieth century, described the church as an unequal society comprising two categories of persons, pastors and flock. It is up to the pastors alone
to guide. 'The one duty of the multitude is to allow themselves
to be led and, like a docile flock, to follows the pastors.'[54] When
people obey in this manner, they do not even have to know
why.

But over the years more people have come to trust in their
own experience. People have discovered their own inner wisdom
and have come to rely on 'the authority of experience'. This is

especially the case where faith has to be applied to the practicalities of daily life. Almost inevitably this has led to a conflict of views. *Humanae Vitae*, the church's teaching on contraception, has become a symbol of this tension between what the church says and people's lived experience.

We are left with a reconfigured relationship between the individual and the church. In the time of 'the experience of authority' conformity was expected. It was a case of 'you fit in with us'. But in the time of 'the authority of experience' this is reversed. People now test the church by the standards of their own inner wisdom. Instead of accepting submissively they ask: Does it make sense? Does it throw light on my living? Will it make me more human?

I am not suggesting we go from the extreme of blind obedience to another extreme of everybody deciding for themselves. But the reconfiguration is happening and some kind of accommodation is indicated. There is needed a new point of intersection, a new space of reconciliation between the individual and the church, where people can feel comfortable in their belonging.

*Critical loyalty*

I suggest the idea of 'critical loyalty' or 'critical belonging' as a term for this space and for what is desirable. It denotes a space where people can be happy to belong – and where the church can be happy for people to be. The term seeks to hold together two 'desirables': a prizing of people's own experience and wisdom; and a prizing of the collective wisdom of the church. Let us take these two in turn.

On the one hand, we need to prize people's wisdom. Adult faith is more than conformity or uniformity or blind obedience. Faith involves a journey. We move beyond childhood faith with its simplifications and its dependence on the thinking of others. This movement will probably include struggle and questioning and doubt. If negotiated well, it will lead to an owned, a chosen faith. As the Samaritans said to the woman who introduced them to Jesus: 'It is no longer because of what you said that we believe, for we have heard for ourselves' (John 4:42).

An owned faith makes up its own mind. It thinks for itself. It continues to question. It explores, pushes the boat out, thinks outside the box. It is creative and imaginative and ever new. If faith is an adult engagement with the mystery of the universe, then this is how it should be. For faith to discover itself in this way, it has to endure the loss of a previous faith.

It would be surprising if such an adult faith were in 100% agreement with everything the church says. Within its overall and larger 'buying-in', one would expect points of questioning, points of dispute, points of dissent. Ideally this adult faith would be welcomed for its questioning and would feel welcome. Otherwise there cannot really be an adult faith.

On the other hand, we need to prize the collective wisdom. Adult faith is more than just an individual 'take', more than just a person's inner wisdom. It is at the same time a kind of contracting in to the collective wisdom. It is respect for a collective wisdom born of two millennia of Christian communities living the mystery. It is a sense of something bigger-than-me, bigger than all of us.

This puts before us another aspect of adult faith. It is humble and docile. I mean 'docile' not in the sense of submissive and compliant, but in the sense of teachable, persuadable, open to learning. Adult faith wants to learn more, to be informed by the collective wisdom, to have its perspectives stretched and challenged.

By collective wisdom I do not mean something fossilised, antiquated, obsolete. It should be about something alive, organic, responsive to the times, ever the same and ever new. Adult faith has a deep appreciation for the riches of such a living tradition. In cases of disagreement, it shows a respectful acquiescence. It allows for the possibility that it may not yet be able to see.

It is these two that 'critical loyalty' holds in tension. Critical loyalty identifies with the core message of Christianity and with the distinctive character of its own particular tradition. It is both humble and questioning, trusting in its inner wisdom and cherishing the collective wisdom. It does not feel compulsion to slavishly adhere to everything. Ideally it feels that the exercise of its critical faculties is welcome.

## À la carte and blind obedience

In this context we might address the phrase 'à la carte Catholic'. It is used in reference to people who, it is felt, pick and choose the bits of Christianity that suit them and leave out the bits that do not. The image is unfair both to individuals and to the church.

Of course such people exist. They reflect the eclectic approach to spirituality that we observe today. But there are many individuals whose deep sense of integrity leaves them both faithful to their church and dissenting from some of its positions. There is nothing whimsical or superficial about their stance. Rather, where they are at may involve a measure of pain for them.

The image also fails to do justice to the church. It lacks any sense of the church as big enough to embrace and accommodate this. It reduces church to a rules-bound, black-and-white, all-or-nothing kind of society, more exclusive than inclusive. (Of course the church itself bears much if not most of the responsibility for the prevalence of this distorted image of itself.)

Also, we must not forget what the culture of blind obedience has done to people in the church. There has been a lot of external conformity, but what lay underneath this? Underneath were large areas where people had no understanding of what they assented to or why. Looking underneath, the conformity is revealed to be uncritical loyalty.

Also, underneath the external conformity, there was often an absence of internal conformity. The culture was one that forced people to suppress their questions, their difficulties, their doubts, their disbelief. I imagine that many in authority would be frightened if people were able to articulate what they actually think, believe, or doubt, about various 'doctrines' of their faith.

*Some distinctions*

I am envisaging a situation where there are diverse views within the church population, and where people may find themselves in disagreement with some of the 'official' positions. The following distinctions may help to show how such diversity and divergence can be embraced.

First there is a distinction between what the church believes and how that belief is expressed. In his opening address to Vatican II, Pope John XXIII distinguished between the doctrines of the church and the different ways in which they are formulated and expressed in different times. So there may be a pluralism of expression, but a unity of belief. The problem is that the actual belief may become identified with a particular expression of it, with the latter mistaken for the former.

For instance, it is a Christian belief that God created the world. But how is this to be explained? Did it happen in the seven days of the Book of Genesis? Or could it be expressed in a way that is compatible with evolutionary theory? Again, there is a Christian belief about peace and violence. Some interpret it as demanding thorough-going pacifism. Others interpret it as allowing for violence in circumscribed conditions (eg the 'just war').

We could get bogged down in the details of any such example. My only concern is to bring out the distinction between, on one hand, the core belief or the core value and, on the other, the particular explanation or interpretation. The distinction helps locate just where the difference lies. Is it that we are we committed to the same belief but differ on the interpretation; or do we differ on the belief itself?

A second distinction concerns what the church calls the 'hierarchy of truths'. According to the Vatican Council, 'In Catholic doctrine there exists an order or "hierarchy" of truths, since they vary in their relation to the foundation of the Christian faith.'[55] For instance the truths that are expressed in the Creed have a centrality compared to other teachings that are not mentioned therein.

This is not to take away from some teachings but simply to say that not everything is on a par. The doctrines of the resurrection and the Trinity are more central than that of papal infallibility. The moral teaching about taking life is more central than that about telling lies. And such moral teachings are more central than church disciplines such as fasting.

Finally, there is a distinction between the local and the universal, expressed in what the church calls the principle of 'subsidiarity'. 'It is an injustice', it says, 'for a larger and higher association to arrogate to itself functions which can be performed efficiently by smaller and lower societies'.[56] This principle expresses a concern about centralisation.

The principle can be applied to the church itself. Some issues are best dealt with at the level of the worldwide church. Other issues are best left to the church in a particular country to work out for their situation. Others again are best left to the individual. Micro-managing people's lives tends to take decisions out of the hands of the individual and the local, and to centralise in an unhealthy way.

*From obedience to fidelity*

I want to spell out now the process of what might be called responsible disagreement. Let us say that you are the person concerned. You are a seriously committed Christian. You have a strong sense of vocation and of mission, of prayer and of belonging. Your difficulties with a specific issue are to be seen in the context of this, your overall fidelity and your contented assent on almost all other matters.

You are a person who appreciates your own fallibility. You question yourself, for you know that you can get it wrong. You know that you have blind spots and that you are subject to bias. You know that 'the spirit of the age' can obscure Christian truths and values. So you come to the teaching of the church with a humble disposition, seeking to listen and to learn.

You know also that the church can get it wrong. You know that the church can become trapped in its own traditions, even thinking them to be of divine origin. You know that there are both church teachings that are prophetic and challenging, and teachings that are archaic and obsolete. You know that is possible for a Christian to faithfully follow a church teaching that is itself not faithful to Christianity.

But you will continue to question. How central to faith is the matter on which I cannot agree? Here the distinctions made above can help. You may also ask: Are there others like me? It is not that numbers prove the truth of any view, but if there is widespread unease on some question, you will ask yourself what that signifies.

In the end, despite all your striving, you are unable to give your sincere intellectual assent, or you are forced to a conflicting conclusion. Notice the word intellectual. This process involves the exercise of the mind; faith is not an irrational activity. Nobody can with integrity give intellectual assent where intellectual conviction is lacking. But the question now is: how can you, in this position, be said to be any less faithful than another person who can give such assent?

In some way such as this, a person may become reconciled with themselves and with their church. They may continue to feel that they belong, not in the sense of blind obedience, but in the sense of critical fidelity. It would be wonderful if the church could make them feel welcome in this way too.

## Public opinion in the church

That leads to my final point. The issue here is not the rights and wrongs of any one teaching. The issue is how people are with one another, especially how the church leadership is with the 'rank-and-file' members. The issue is about how things are decided rather than what is decided.

The church has a place in its processes for what it calls consultation. For instance it says that diocesan and parish councils have a consultative role, and that the advice of those consulted should normally be followed. Many wish that there were more than consultation, that people would have more of a say in decisions. But let us see how far we can take this theme of consultation. It has more significance than might appear.

People can be suspicious when they are consulted about something. They want to know what is going to happen when they give their view. They wonder if they are being taken seriously. People know that to consult with your mind already made up is a lie. To consult and then not to listen is a betrayal. Consultation in its deep, spiritual meaning is a serious commitment. Consultation is a search for the truth.

The ultimate purpose of consultation is that we would hear God's Spirit, the Spirit of truth. We know that the Spirit can speak through any of us. Therefore it is only when we listen genuinely to each person that we can be sure of hearing the Spirit and arriving at the truth. When the church recommends consultation, that is what is involved.

This calls the church to move from a culture of conformity to a culture of public opinion. I mean a culture where it matters what people think, where listening is vital, where viewpoints are valued, where diversity is enriching, where feedback is important. A culture of public opinion is seen as the path into deeper truth. Unlike a culture of uniformity and conformity, there is no fear of the truth.

When there is the tension of disagreement, some will continue to belong, in a spirit of critical loyalty, but others will take their leave. Hopefully their retiring from church will not be their departing from discipleship. Maybe there is also a form of belonging 'from a distance'.

*For reflection*
Reflect on some teaching you think the church is wrong about. Reflect on some teaching you have come to appreciate. Reflect on some teaching you do not understand. How would you describe the quality of your own belonging?

CHAPTER THIRTY

## *Being Thankful*

The theme of thanks has come up a few times during this book. I return to the theme as a conclusion to these chapters of section three, on 'Living the Life'. It seems to me that thankfulnesss is at the heart of living the life and that it expresses the hope-filled spirit of Christian living. It is remarkable that thanksgiving (Eucharist) is the name we choose for the central act of the Christian community.

The thankfulness of a Christian is a very distinctive approach to living. It is a distinctive way of seeing the events of daily life and of responding to them. I will elaborate on this by first contrasting the two words 'fate' and 'providence'.

*Fate*
Some people look at events in life in terms of fate. Things are said to happen for a reason. Fate is about things being destined to happen. They are not accidental, but preordained, perhaps by some divinity, and they will unfold with inevitability. There is little freedom here. We can cry out but we cannot alter the predetermined course of events. Things are 'meant to be'.

We say, for instance, that such a person was 'fated to suffer' or 'fated to succeed'. We say about some series of events that 'It couldn't have been otherwise.' We say about somebody: 'From the moment he was born you could see that ...' There is a sense in all this of a puppeteer on the other side of the curtain. Things are being played out and we have no access to the controls. Sometimes we resort to different means such as astrology in an effort to discern patterns.

The phrase 'the will of God' sometimes fits with this mentality. The phrase came up in the discussions of suffering and of Jesus' death on the cross. When we say that some event is God's will, we are trying to believe that 'it didn't just happen', that there was a reason. Again there is that sense of the inscrutable puppeteer.

Maybe both the mindset of 'fate' and that of 'God's will' come to the same thing. They help to give people a sense of order. But in the process, they make for unsatisfying views of the world and of God and of ourselves. We are too much at the mercy of forces we do not understand; too much manipulation and very little freedom.

The opposite option would be something like blind chance. In this view there is no order or pattern. World events are ruled by randomness. Things just happen, anything can happen, you just get on with it and learn to live with the chaos. When believers think on these lines, it is as if they believe that God made the world and then forgot about it.

### Providence

None of this corresponds to the Christian view of reality. Rather, as proposed earlier, in creating the world God created evolution. God set in train a gigantic process of evolution, of which we are but one tiny moment. But God stays with the process. The evolving creation is imbued with Spirit; God's accompanying Spirit, God's passion for the world's becoming.

The becoming or evolving is open, free. Whatever happens is neither predetermined nor blind chance. What happens occurs in accord with the inbuilt tendencies and possibilities of creation. What happens is sometimes orderly and sometimes chaotic. That is the kind of process it is. And a lot of what happens is the result of human freedom, whether exercised for good or for bad.

So things do happen for reasons but not for preordained reasons. Events could always have been otherwise. Maybe, within a process, once 'A' happens, then 'B' and 'C' are inevitable, or almost inevitable. But 'A' itself could have been otherwise. And even if we say that all of human history, past and future, is equally present to God, we cannot say that tomorrow is already decided.

Christianity sees further into all this and that is where the word 'providence' comes in. St Paul says: 'For those who love God, everything works together for the good' (Romans 8:28). What I take the words to mean is that those who are attuned to the God of Jesus Christ find a providence in things. The words are about how Christians see. They are about the shape or pattern their seeing gives to events.

'Being attuned to the God of Jesus Christ.' I am referring here to the cross and resurrection of Jesus. This is where we find laid bare the pattern and dynamic of God's creation. It is a resurrection pattern, a pattern of transformation, a pattern of breaking through into further, higher spheres of existence. The pattern is God's ever-present 'making all things new' (Revelation 21:5).

This is providence, the pattern that God has, as it were, provided for the evolving creation. It is not about inevitabilities but about possibilities. To believe in the God who raised Jesus from the dead is to accept an invitation to see all of reality from the vantage-point of resurrection and transformation. This does not mean that every event necessarily leads to transformation. It means that transformation can be found in any event. All things can work together for the good.

For example, when we look back on our lives, we see how events can change their meaning. Something is experienced at the time as a disaster. Yet, months maybe years later, we may look back on it and see blessing. What seemed to be only misfortune becomes part of a bigger picture. It is not automatic or inevitable. It is about the way we come to see the event differently than we did at the time.

Repentance is another example. What is wrong is wrong but it can also become part of a bigger picture and a better story. At the time, the wrongdoing is experienced as failure. But with time we can look back and see that it was the gateway to growth. The wrong we did is no longer the last word on who we are. With repentance it leads into a new chapter, to become an element in a new story.

## Thankfulness

It is said that 10% of life is what happens to us and that 90% is how we deal with it. For the Christian, the 90% is about seeing things in terms of providence, from a resurrection perspective. It is where we come from; it is what we bring to the situation. Another way of putting this is to say that Christianity is about seeing things thankfully.

I do not mean that, when something bad happens, we are thankful because something bad happens. That would be perverted. Rather, Christians have thankful hearts. They are thankful for the basic structure of existence as laid bare in Jesus' death and resurrection. They are thankful that all of reality is an invitation into transformation, an invitation into new spheres of existence. There is nothing that is outside this. It determines how Christians see everything.

So even the bad things are seen from the standpoint of a thankful heart. It is the same spirit as Jesus' at his last supper, facing his impending death, taking bread and giving thanks. It is the spirit in which Paul proclaimed: 'If God is for us, who is against us?' (Romans 8:31). Seeing things in this thankful way means seeing them differently, seeing them with eyes of hope.

It is far from being a glib attitude, for it comes with a price. A thankful heart must learn to see things differently. It has to overcome its own temptation to give in and to despair. It has to find the hope. Most of all, it has to translate its way of seeing into a thankful, hope-filled way of living. This is demanded by the kind of faith Christianity is, by its convictions about the kind of God that God is.

Somebody said: It is not happiness that makes us grateful, but gratitude that makes us happy. A Christian, someone who is in touch with what Christianity is, learns to be thankful. This in turn changes everything else. A constant disposition of gratitude leaves us available for the grace in life. It leaves us disposed, ready, available to see the grace in everything. This sense is captured in the culminating scene of the story and film, *Babette's Feast*:

> But the moment comes when our eyes are opened, and we see and realise that grace is infinite. Grace, my friends, demands nothing from us but that we shall await it with confidence and acknowledge it in gratitude.[57]

*Eucharist*

Gratitude-grace-Eucharist. It is the same root word: grace, thanksgiving. We return to the last supper, to 'Do this in memory of me.' Again we hear Jesus, as he breaks the bread, giving thanks. We recognise him in the breaking of bread and we know that thankfulness is what life is all about.

The letter to the Colossians says: 'Let the peace of Christ rule in your hearts, to which indeed you were called in the one body. And be thankful' (3:15). 'Be thankful' translates the Greek *eucharistoi ginesthe*. It is the word Eucharist; it might be rendered 'show yourselves to be eucharistic'. That is what is asked of any-body who would 'Do this in memory of me.'

*For reflection*
What difference does it make when you live life from a disposi-tion of gratitude?

# References

1. *Page 24:* Martel, Yann, *The Life of Pi* (Edinburgh: Canongate, 2002), p 28.
2. *Page 35:* Augustine, Sermon 150:2.
3. *Page 47:* Lyons, Enda, *Jesus: Self-Portrait by God* (Dublin: Columba, 1994).
4. *Page 55:* Davie, Grace, *Religion in Britain since 1945* (Oxford: Wiley-Blackwell, 1994).
5. *Page 56:* Vatican II, *Constitution on the Church in the Modern World (Gaudium et Spes)*, paragraph 19.
6. *Page 66:* Augustine, Sermon 57:7.
7. *Page 67:* John Paul II, *For the Year of the Eucharist (Mane Nobiscum Domine)*, 2004, paragraph 24.
8. *Page 71:* Merton, Thomas, *Conjectures of a Guilty Bystander* (New York: Image Books, 1968), p 158.
9. *Page 71:* Shakespeare, William, *All's Well That Ends Well*, IV, 3:83-87.
10. *Page 75:* Newman, John Henry, *Apologia Pro Vita Sua* (1886. London: Oxford University Press, 1964), p 252.
11. *Page 76:* Augustine, Sermon 167:1.
12. *Page 88:* Augustine, Sermon 117:5.
13. *Page 93:* Author Unknown, *The Cloud of Unknowing*, 4 and 6.
14. *Page 105:* Augustine, Sermon 171:2.
15. *Page 105:* Rahner, Karl, 'Why does God allow us to suffer?' *Theological Investigations Volume 19* (London: Darton, Longman & Todd, 1984), p 206.
16. *Page 106:* Pope Leo XII, *Rerum Novarum* (1891), paragraph 14.
17. *Page 106:* Metz, Johann Baptist, *Faith in History and Society* (London: Burns & Oates, 1980), chapters 5, 6 and 11.
18. *Page 111:* Shakespeare, William, *The Tempest*, I, 2:397-399.
19. *Page 113:* Augustine, Sermon 170:9.
20. *Page 113:* Augustine, Sermon 170:9.
21. *Page 113:* Augustine, Sermon 159:1.
22. *Page 114:* Augustine, Sermon 84:2.
23. *Page 114:* Augustine, Sermon 229B:2.
24. *Page 115:* Listz, Franz, *Preface to Les Prèludes*.

25. *Page 116:* Congregation for the Doctrine of the Faith, Declaration *Dominus Iesus* (2000), paragraph 22.
26. *Page 117:* Vatican II, *Constitution on the Church (Lumen Gentium)*, paragraph 16.
27. *Page 118:* Merton, Thomas, *Conjectures of a Guilty Bystander* (New York: Doubleday / Image Books, 1968), p 44.
28. *Page 128:* Augustine, Sermon 72A:7-8.
29. *Page 136:* John Paul II, *On the Vocation and Mission of the Lay Faithful (Christifideles Laici,* 1988), paragraph 11.
30. *Page 136:* Guzie, Tad, *The Book of Sacramental Basics* (New York: Paulist, 1981), p 78.
31. *Page 139:* Newman, John Henry, *Parochial and Plain Sermons;* quoted in A.N. Wilson (editor), *John Henry Newman: Prayers, Poems, Meditations* (London: SPCK, 1989), p 99.
32. *Page 140: Catechism of the Catholic Church,* paragraph 1547.
33. *Page 142:* Pope Paul VI, *Evangelisation in the Modern World (Evagelii Nuntiandi,* 1975), paragraph 24.
34. *Page 146:* Vatican II, *Constitution on the Liturgy (Sacrosanctum Concilium)*, paragraph 10.
35. *Page 147:* Barry, Sebastian, *The Secret Scripture* (London: Faber and Faber, 2008), p 38.
36. *Page 147:* Williams, Rowan, *Sermon at Lourdes, 24 September 2008* (quoted in *The Tablet,* 27 September 2008, p 39).
37. *Page 150:* Davie, Grace, 'Is Europe an Exceptional Case?' *The Hedgehog Review,* Spring-Summer 2006, p 24
38. *Page 153:* This and following quotations from Augustine, Sermon 272.
39. *Page 158:* This and following quotations from T. S. Eliot, *Four Quartets,* the first quartet, 'Burnt Norton'.
40. *Page 163:* Newman, John Henry, *The Dream of Gerontius,* part 3.
41. *Page 168:* Augustine, Letter 130.22; Sermon 56:4.
42. *Page 168:* Augustine, Sermon 59:8.
43. *Page 168:* Augustine, Sermon 154A:6.
44. *Page 169: Catechism of the Catholic Church,* paragraph 2739.
45. *Page 171:* Cervantes, *Don Quixote,* part 2, chapter 55.
46. *Page 172:* Vatican II, *Constitution on Divine Revelation (Dei Verbum)*, paragraph 21.
47. *Page 173:* Augustine, Sermon 56.10; 58.5

48. *Page 176:* Augustine, Sermon 171.2.

49. *Page 176:* Augustine, Sermon 122.1

50. *Page 177:* Ricoeur, Paul, 'The Hermeneutical Function of Distanciation', *Hermeneutics and the Human Sciences* (Cambridge University Press, 1981), p 143.

51. *Page 179:* Eliot, T.S. *Four Quartets*, 'The Dry Salvages'.

52. *Page 185:* Fairlie, Henry, *The Seven Deadly Sins Today* (New York: Simon & Schuster, 1978), p 5.

53. *Page 191:* Vatican II, *Constitution on the Church in the Modern World (Gaudium et Spes)*, paragraph 39.

54. *Page 204:* Pope Pius X, *Vehementer* (1906), paragraph 8.

55. *Page 208:* Vatican Council, *Decree on Ecumenism (Unitatis Redintegratio)*, paragraph 11.

56. *Page 208:* Pope Pius XI, *Quadragesimo Anno* (1931), paragraph 79.

57. *Page 215:* Isak Dinesen, 'Babette's Feast', *Anecdotes of Destiny* (1958; London: Penguin, 1986), p 60.